The Union Of Bliss And Emptiness

The Union Of Bliss And Emptiness

A Commentary on the Lama Choepa Guru Yoga Practice

H.H. the Dalai Lama, Tenzin Gyatso

Translated by Thupten Jinpa

Snow Lion Publications
Ithaca, New York

Snow Lion Publications
P.O. Box 6483
Ithaca, New York 14851
USA

Printed in USA.

ISBN 0-937938-69-6

Library of Congress Cataloging-in-Publication Data

Bstan-'dzin-rgya-mtsho, Dalai Lama XIV, 1935–
    The union of bliss and emptiness.

    Bibliography: p.
    Includes index.
        1. Blo-bzaṅ-chos-kyi-rgyal-mtshan, Panchen Lama I,
1567?-1662. Bla ma mchod pa'i cho ga.   2. Guru
worship (Rite)—Buddhism—China—Tibet.   3. Buddhism—
China—Tibet—Doctrines.   I. Thupten Jinpa.   II. Title.
BQ7699.G87B79   1988   294.3'4448   88-31948
ISBN 0-937938-69-6

Contents

Preface

Guru yoga is an important aspect of the tantric practice of mahayana buddhism and the foundation on which the whole tantric structure is built; it is also the force that gives vitality to a serious practitioner's meditation. Unlike other systems, tantric meditation depends largely upon inspiration transmitted in an unbroken lineage through a living person, the guru. Practitioners should first be initiated into the discipline through an empowerment ceremony that makes their mental continuum receptive to the intricate meditative techniques of tantra, following which they should be led through the successive stages of the path by an expert guide.

This book presents a practical instruction which blends the essential aspects of the sutra path together with the profound tantric techniques that activate the latent spiritual forces within us. By laying the basic framework of the entire buddhist path, it also sets down the guidelines for undertaking a complete form of practice on a daily basis.

The lucidity and the liveliness of His Holiness the Fourteenth Dalai Lama's commentary make such meditation a most inspiring and gratifying practice. His Holiness has defined and underlined the great importance of guru yoga practice as follows: "Guru yoga is not just a practice where one visualizes

8

a deity and then makes seven-limbed offerings, but rather it
is where one views one's own root guru as a real buddha from
the depths of one's heart. Having cultivated such an attitude
and strong faith, one then engages in actually pleasing the guru
by following his advice. It is through such a method that one
should try to achieve a transference of the guru's realizations
to one's own mental continuum. Such a practice is called guru
yoga.''

The root text *Sablam Lama Choepai Choga Detong Yerme-
ma* (A Method of Offering to the Guru, The Profound Path
Entitled the Indivisibility of Bliss and Emptiness) by Panchen
Lozang Choekyi Gyaltsen and an oral commentary by His Holiness the Fourteenth Dalai Lama are translated here. The teaching was given at Dharamsala by His Holiness in March 1986,
at the Second Enlightenment Experience Celebration organized
by the Foundation for the Preservation of the Mahayana Tradition. The transcript of the simultaneous English translation
was then checked thoroughly with the Tibetan and amended
with necessary corrections by the translator. Since the commentary given by His Holiness was an experiential one, tradition requires four repetitions of the major sections of the text.
These have been incorporated into the main body of the teaching for the present book, and a few brief footnotes, together
with a bibliography of books mentioned in the text, have been
provided.

Grateful thanks are due to Ven. Alfred Luyens for transcrib-
ing, to Nerea and Paloma for typing, and to Christine Cox,
for final editing. Special thanks go to the initial editor who
devoted months of work to this project, but who wishes to remain anonymous. The text used herein is a compilation based
on the translations of Dr. Alexander Berzin and Ven. Martin
Willson.

Although I have tried to make the translation as close to the
original and as correct as possible, due to my limited experience
and knowledge some errors may have remained undetected.
For these and all other shortcomings I request the readers'
forgiveness.

Through the merit that has been accumulated by this translation, may all sentient beings enjoy the great fortune of coming under the perfect and compassionate spiritual guidance of His Holiness the Dalai Lama.

THUPTEN JINPA
Gaden Shartse College, 1988

1 Introduction

The origins of the instructions on this *Lama Choepa* practice are traced back to the explanatory tantra called *Vajramala*, in which the visualization of the body mandala deities on the guru's body is explained according to Guhyasamaja. Since the integral practice of the three deities Yamantaka, Guhyasamaja and Heruka has great merit and advantages, *Lama Choepa* explains how to do it on the basis of this guru yoga practice. The actual practice is explained on the basis of Guhyasamaja, the preliminaries such as the self-generation are explained on the basis of Yamantaka, and the performing of offerings and so forth is explained according to Heruka. This guru yoga is widespread within the Gelug system—so much so that almost everyone knows it by heart—and the way in which it is undertaken is uniform. In other traditions, there are different ways of practicing guru yoga, such as the system of Ngor of the Sakya tradition, and others.

Having achieved this precious human form and having received initiation, you should observe the vows and commitments properly and engage in the tantric path in order to actualize the resultant state endowed with the seven features of the deity and his consort facing each other.[1] The method for achieving this is explained by Panchen Lama Lozang Choekyi

Gyaltsen[2] in the last stanza of *Lama Choepa*:

HAVING BEEN THUS ENTREATED, PRAY GRANT
THIS REQUEST, O SUPREME GURUS:
SO THAT YOU MIGHT BLESS ME, HAPPILY
ALIGHT ON THE CROWN OF MY HEAD
AND ONCE AGAIN SET YOUR RADIANT FEET
FIRMLY
AT THE COROLLA OF MY HEART LOTUS.

One must fervently pray to the guru by taking guru yoga practice as the life of the path; through this practice and the path one can actualize the pure illusory body[3] and the meaning clear light,[4] the factors that lead the practitioners to the resultant buddhahood. Therefore, the followers of Lama Tsongkhapa traditionally take the practice of guru yoga as the life of the path and undertake a practice which integrates the three deities Guhyasamaja, Yamantaka and Heruka.

The meditational deity Yamantaka is the wrathful aspect of Manjushri. Generally, Manjushri is regarded as being the father, the mother and also the son of the buddhas. Manjushri has arisen into a wrathful aspect called Yamantaka because, during the initial stage of practice, factors such as one's mental faculties, accumulation of merits, force of effort, favorableness of conditions and so forth are very weak; hence, there are more unfavorable conditions and adverse circumstances. At these levels even a slight obstacle can cause great harm to the practitioner. The special significance of Yamantaka practice is that on the basis of increasing the wisdom realizing emptiness one will be guarded from the external and internal obstacles. Therefore the practice of Yamantaka is important.

The practice of Guhyasamaja is regarded as the actual path. There are two major systems or schools of Guhyasamaja, known as the Arya school and the Janapata school, both of which evolved in India. Within the Arya system there are many divisions, according with the specific central deity of the mandala. The main one is the Guhyasamaja Akshobhya; Nagarjuna wrote many treatises on this, including a very profound text on the generation stage called *Pindikrita Sadhana* (Condensation of the Means of Accomplishment), which outlines the practice of taking the three bodies[5] into the path. It expounds the main theme of the Guhyasamaja root tantra based on the interpretation of the explanatory tantra *Vajramala*. To give an example, the process of withdrawing the "specially imagined deities" during the stage of taking death into the path as the truth body is explained very well in conjunction with the process of dissolution of the twenty-five gross phenomena.[6] This practice has an added advantage when one subsequently arises into the enjoyment body, the primordial being, through the order of the five clarifications, the *adhisambodhis*.[7] There are various instructions on the meditation on the three kayas, as outlined in many different sadhanas, and although all of them contain the important features in complete form and serve the same purpose, they also have their individual significance.

Since Guhyasamaja emphasizes the practice of the illusory body, it has a very unique practice for taking the intermediate state into the path as the enjoyment body. By comparison, in practices such as Heruka, although the practice of taking the intermediate state into the path as the enjoyment body is explained, it is done implicitly on the basis of visualizing syllables and hand symbols within the channels. In the practice of Yamantaka, when one takes the intermediate state into the path as the enjoyment body, the practice of what is called the causal vajraholder is explained, wherein one generates as Manjushri. But when one actually arises into the illusory body during the completion stage, it is in Yamantaka form. However, there is another view asserting that the practitioner arises into Manjushri at the completion stage just as he has rehearsed during the generation stage. In Heruka, although one generates as a *nada* (channel) during the generation stage, which serves the purpose of being a ripening factor for the completion state, one actually arises in the form of Heruka lord and consort at the completion stage.

So, although in such tantras as Heruka and Yamantaka the techniques for actualizing the illusory body are explained, there they are considered more as ripening factors. The actual practice is done on the basis of visualizing channels and syllables and so forth. But in Guhyasamaja, as explained by Nagarjuna in his *Pindikrita Sadhana*, taking the intermediate state into the path as the enjoyment body is done on the basis of oneself arising into the primordial buddha. This is a ripening factor which is similar in feature to the actual illusory body of the completion stage, the difference being only the presence or absence of a consort. This similarity would be of great advantage during the stages of the three isolations[8] and of the illusory body itself, because one arises into the form of the very deity with which one has cultivated great familiarity on the generation stage. Even during the generation stage this has a special significance, because the most important part of the generation stage is the practice of the three bodies. This shows that the practice of Guhyasamaja is the foundation.

In order to have proper, or highest, fulfillment of the practice of the three bodies—that is, realization of the completion stage—it is necessary to have the experience of clear light, and this has to be induced by generating bliss within one's continuum. The techniques for generating bliss have been explained in the Heruka root tantra. The process for melting the bodhicitta at the crown and experiencing the four joys at specific parts of the body, as explained in Heruka, is unique. When the bodhicitta, the source of great bliss, melts, it flows down to the vital points of the body where specific mantra circles have been visualized, and lingers for a while. Thus one obtains special power to increase the experience of great bliss and bring about a stable experience of clear light. The force of this inner yoga could also have an effect during the meeting with a suitable and qualified consort. So one enriches one's practice of the three bodies through Heruka, and thus it helps to make one's practice more complete; it also accelerates one's realizations. Therefore, the practice of Heruka is taken as an assisting factor to one's practice of Guhyasamaja. Guhyasamaja is like the actual path, Heruka the assisting factor and Yamantaka, as a preliminary, the force for overcoming obstacles. So, if these three were to be practiced in an integrated way with the knowledge of their individual unique features, it would be good. But the real meaning of undertaking the practice of these three deities inseparably comes during the completion stage.

In addition, all these practices have to be undertaken on the basis of taking guru yoga as the life of the path. Since the guru is the supreme field of merit, there is a guru yoga at the beginning of almost all the sadhanas of the Indian masters. This indicates the importance of guru yoga practice. In a deeper sense, even the practice of the three bodies is essentially a guru yoga practice, because during the entire meditation one views the meditational deity as inseparable from the guru. Nevertheless, when one undertakes the practice of accumulating merit and purifying negativities specifically on the basis of guru yoga, it has a very special power; hence the sadhanas have separate practices of guru yoga at the beginning.

Although such is the case, in Tibet guru yoga practice was so widespread and so much emphasized that there are certain manuals exclusively devoted to it. This is the case in each of the four main sects of Tibetan buddhism. There are many different manuals, such as this text, *Lama Choepa*, each of which presents a variation of guru yoga practice. Their significance, or necessity, is that one has to train in such a path in order to moisten one's dry mind and tame it through receiving the guru's blessings. But I think that the mere recitation of the words of a text alone cannot tame our minds; this requires inspiration which has to come through a living force in the form of a guru. Although meditational deities have great power, and also the buddhas have high qualities, we do not have the ability to see them and they are not directly accessible to us. But the complete transmissions of both the profound and vast practices have been given to us in an unbroken lineage, which starts from Lord Buddha himself, by our root gurus. Among the root gurus that we have, there might be ordinary beings, bodhisattvas and so forth, but irrespective of what they might be from their side, on our part we have to view them as actual Vajradharas, and the source of inspiration. We will receive blessings and inspiration according to how well we are able to base our practice on such a view. Therefore, the practice of guru yoga is extremely important. When a follower of Gelug does a guru yoga practice, it is very helpful and it has special significance if it is done on the basis of seeing one's own root guru as inseparable from Lama Tsongkhapa.

I think that in India there was no manual exclusively for guru yoga practice, although you will find in many Indian sadhanas a guru yoga at the beginning, for the purpose of accumulating merit. In Tibet, however, there are many guru yoga practices. In the Gelug system there is one called *Khedup Chikyue* (The Solo LIneage Through Khedup Rinpoche) which is very much related to manuals on emptiness meditation, and one through Jetsun Sherab Senge called *Gaden Lhagyama* (The Hundred Deities of the Joyous Land) from the Segyu lineage. These are very integrated guru yoga practices but do not require the receiving of initiation into highest yoga tantra. There is also one through Togden Jampael Gyatso and Baso Choekyi Gyaltsen known as the *Ear-Whispered Transmission*. The latter is the lineage of *Lama Choepa*. The most widely known guru yogas related to Lama Tsongkhapa are this *Lama Choepa* and the *Gaden Lhagyama*. There might also be other lineages of guru yogas, but the above three are the most popularly known. Among these various guru yoga lineages, *Lama Choepa* is very profound and comprehensive; its practice requires initiation into the highest yoga tantra.

For practitioners like ourselves who have not gained complete realization of the common path, but through the kindness of the guru have been fortunate enough to have received high initiations, and also have access to the practice of guru yoga related to tantra, it would be very good to engage in the practices of lamrim, lojong (thought transformation) and guru yoga, and also the practices of generation stage and completion stage, all in relation to *Lama Choepa* practice. In this practice one first generates oneself into the deity, thus countering ordinary conception and appearance, then visualizes the merit field followed by the mandala deities on the body of the guru. As stated above, the general framework of this text is guru yoga as explained in the tantras: this practice contains the unique features of the tantric path such as the meditation on the four complete purities.[9] The essential points of the generation stage, such as the three bodies, are explained, as are the essential points of the completion stage. The text also discusses the main aspects of the common path, such as the practices of the three scopes, and the essential points of the thought transformation practices. Hence it is a very vast and integrated practice. *Lama Choepa* has an uninterrupted transmission of inspiration, and yet it is very easy to practice. It has been the main practice of many great masters of the past. Of all the guru yogas, the one which contains all the essential points of both sutra and tantra is this text.

Generally speaking, if one has the proper understanding, even the shortest guru yoga will give one a complete understanding of the paths. But if one does not have the proper understanding, even though one might read the entire eight thousand verses of *Prajnaparamita* (Perfection of Wisdom), for example, one will not understand it. In this popular guru yoga known as *Lama Choepa*, the verses explicitly deal with the most essential points of lamrim and tantric practices.

As Lama Tsongkhapa said in *Yonten Shigyurma* (The Foundation of All Excellences):

> The foundation of all the perfections is the kind guru.
> Having seen that proper reliance on him
> is the root and basis of all the paths,
> Inspire me to relate to him with every effort.

and:

> Bless me to gain realization of the main points
> of the two stages,[10] the essence of the tantric path;
> And, by never wavering from the yoga of four sessions,
> achieve the realizations as taught by the sages.

In order to achieve nirvana or enlightenment, one has to depend upon an experienced and qualified master who is able to show the proper and correct path for the achievement of such a resultant state. The actual mode of the practice of the path has been explained in many sutras and tantras using various skillful methods. If one is able to place oneself under the care of such a spiritual master, there is a great advantage—one will make the most progress on the path and overcome all obstacles. Therefore, to develop a correct practice one has to rely upon a qualified master and follow his instructions to the word. In order for one to achieve highest enlightenment, the guru is an indispensable factor; therefore the Buddha explained the qualifications one's master should have, beginning with those outlined in the vinaya. One entrusts oneself to the care of a spiritual master, and will take vows and so on from him or her, so such a person has to be viewed as a buddha. This has also been stated in the treatises of the bodhisattvas. Similarly, it has been explained in the lower tantras and especially in highest yoga tantra that one has to view the guru as the actual embodiment of all the buddhas, the meditational deities and all the refuges, because he is the source, or the great door through which one can experience the blessings and inspiration of the Three Jewels. Therefore, guru yoga practice is the life of all practices. It is important in sutra and especially in tantric practices. One must understand that the practice of guru yoga lays the foundation for the practice of highest yoga tantra. It is also the main practice for accumulating merit and overcoming obstacles. Although it is virtuous and creates a lot of merit to meditate on many different deities, one gains more merit by meditating on the meditational deity as inseparable from the guru. In order to undertake such a practice, one must have trained in the common paths and have been ripened through proper initiations and have accumulated all the necessary articles for practice.

The guru can be visualized in many ways, but according to the guru yoga of *Lama Choepa*, one first visualizes him in front of oneself, then at one's crown and finally descending down to one's heart. Hence this practice contains the essential points of each of these three ways of visualizing the guru.

Guru yoga practice lays down the foundations for a proper path and practice. Also in his *Jhangchub Lamrim Chenmo* (Great Exposition of the Stages of The Path), Lama Tsongkhapa says that proper reliance on the guru is "the root of all the paths." The process of relying on a guru is divided into two: relying through the mind and through actions. "Relying through the mind" refers mainly to establishing the bases: cultivating strong faith in the guru and cultivating respect for him by reflecting upon his great kindness. These have to be developed through reasoning, by seeing the indispensability of the guru for the achievement of highest enlightenment. Relying "through action" means living one's life according to the advice of the teacher. It also involves making offerings and services to him.

If you are able to develop a heartfelt faith and conviction in your guru by reflecting upon his great qualifications and viewing him as a true buddha, this will be of great advantage for cultivating a very receptive mind, fertile for spiritual progress on the path. The stronger your faith, the more progress you will make in your practice. In regard to ordinary persons, the more one respects and feels close to someone, the more readily one will follow his suggestions; so, in the same way, the more faith one has in one's guru, the more progress one will make in one's practice.

The treatises of sutra and tantra are the straightedge by which the directness of the path is determined, and the disciples should be accordingly led on the path by the guru. If there are no proper qualifications on the part of the guru, and also if the student is always infested with doubts, hesitations and so forth and does not relate to the guru in the proper way, there is hardly any possibility for progress on the path.

It is the general nature of the minds of human beings of this time that when one thinks of unwholesome deeds one's mind is very sharp, alert, clever and inventive, but when one focuses on the dharma it does not retain such force and quality. Irrespective of the state of consciousness or awareness of our society in general, as far as we as individuals are concerned, we can judge our own ability to overcome sufferings by our own presently poor nature. Therefore, it is important that we should hope, and on the basis of a new method, one which we have not tried so far and with which we have not been familiar in past lives, we should seek for ways by which we can free ourselves and also other sentient beings from this cycle of existence. Although we have many relatives and friends whom we trust and to whom we relate very closely, such as our parents, none of them have the capacity to guide us on the proper path to the final achievement of enlightenment. It is only the guru who can show the path correctly.

You should recall the fact that all the buddhas of the past initially cultivated bodhicitta for the sake of other sentient beings, then engaged in the practice of the actual path, and at the resultant stage achieved the highest enlightenment, all for the sake of other sentient beings. One will find that it is one's own guru who shows one the various skillful means for bringing about the resultant state of omniscience within one's mental continuum. If the buddhas are engaged in helping all sentient beings, including oneself, it is definitely only through the guru that they perform these activities. Therefore, the guru is the only door through which we benefit from the activities of the buddhas. It would be rather odd if it were the case that a buddha, who has achieved all realizations, when actually helping sentient beings would have to depend on an ordinary being. Therefore you should view the guru as the embodiment of the Buddha, irrespective of whether he is a buddha in reality or not. As far as oneself is concerned, one's root guru is the most kind and most valuable. Although Lord Buddha is sacred and a very high being, as far as we are concerned we did not have the fortune to see him in person; the same with Nagarjuna: although he had tremendous wisdom, we did not see him.

When you rely on a qualified guru it is necessary to have proper reliance. The importance of this has been outlined in both sutra and tantra. Because of its extreme importance, it has been emphasized repeatedly. Especially in highest yoga tantra, the gravity of seeing one's guru and the deity as separate is mentioned many times. In the treatises of tantra it is said that whenever one engages in its practice, one has to overcome ordinary appearance and conception; therefore, when one relates to the guru one has to prevent the ordinary appearance and apprehension of the guru from arising. It is thus very important to undertake guru yoga practice with divine pride and pure divine appearance.

Lama Tsongkhapa was a great scholar and also very highly realized; among the multitudes of eminent personalities of Tibet, his status as a great scholar and meditator is unparalleled. As Gungtang Rinpoche said in his *Geden Tenpa Gyepai Monlam* (A Prayer for the Flourishing of Virtuous Doctrine):

> You are a great scholar rich in vast knowledge,
> A practitioner integrating what you learned into your mental stream,
> A noble being, dedicating all the merits for the dharma and beings;
> May the tradition of Victorious Lozang flourish always.

He received many teachings and did much practice, and also dedicated all his virtues for the flourishing of the dharma. It is not necessary for me to relate here the greatness of his scholarship and the contributions he made to buddhism in Tibet. Lama Tsongkhapa's works run into eighteen volumes. They are very popular and stand as a testimony to his greatness. Among the eighteen there are certain miscellaneous works related to rituals such as for making rain and so forth, but otherwise all these volumes present very profound aspects of the doctrine. They all have their source in authentic Indian works, and the profound aspects of buddhist doctrine, especially the most difficult points, have been analyzed in them using numerous logical processes. This is a fact which we can see for ourselves.

Lama Tsongkhapa came from Amdo, and when he was very young he went to central Tibet. He was not already like a buddha when he was a child. Irrespective of whether he was a manifestation of Manjushri or not, it is better to view him as being born an ordinary person, becoming like Manjushri through so much effort and practice; this will give you more encouragement. It shows us that we can understand something that we have not previously understood, and achieve something not realized before. For some persons it is different: for them it is more inspiring when someone is said to be an embodiment of Nagarjuna or Manjushri and so on right from birth—but I feel more inspired when someone was ordinary at the beginning. So, although Lama Tsongkhapa might be the manifestation of Manjushri, since he took an ordinary form we should rather view him as being an ordinary person at the time of his birth. He did everything that is necessary for a normal monk. He became a great scholar and became highly realized. And his followers, popularly known as the new school of Kadam, made a great contribution to the doctrine of Buddha in Tibet.

The unique quality of the Gelugpas is that they are followers of Lama Tsongkhapa and have a system for very thorough and detailed study, not only of sutra but also of tantra, right from the beginning. And after having engaged in such detailed and thorough studies, one should put them into practice. Having to enter the first path, the path of accumulation, at the beginning is common to all the four sects of Tibetan buddhism. However, because the Gelug tradition has the unique system of undertaking thorough and detailed study encompassing the entire range of the philosophy, I think it has more advantages due to providing one with more avenues of reasoning when one sits down to meditate. The wider one's study has been, the wider one's perspective will be; hence the meditation will be more powerful in bringing about transformation of the mind.

As Lama Tsongkhapa said at the end of *Yonten Shigyurma*:

> In all my lives may I never be parted
> From perfect gurus and always enjoy the glory of dharma;

And having realized the paths and grounds,
May I quickly attain the Vajradhara state.

We have obtained this precious human form and met with
the dharma and also are in the care of a spiritual master of
the mahayana lineage. At this juncture, when we have this great
opportunity and the right conditions, we should make an effort to use them meaningfully. On that basis, you should seek
at best to achieve highest enlightenment; if you cannot, you
should try to achieve enlightenment during the intermediate
state in dependence on the highest yoga tantra path; otherwise, you should try to achieve enlightenment over several future lifetimes. The foundation of all these is the proper reliance on the guru, both mentally and through actions. This
is the actual, the practical, foundation of the path. As for us,
who are practitioners of highest yoga tantra, the root guru,
who is kind in three ways,[11] should be seen as inseparable from
the meditational deity. This will give a special power to our
practice.

What follows is a very brief "experiential" commentary on
the *Lama Choepa* guru yoga. You should cultivate the motivation: I shall read this guru yoga commentary not only for
my own sake but for the sake of all the other sentient beings.
Your motivation should be influenced by at least a simulated
bodhicitta, the altruistic aspiration to attain complete enlightenment for the benefit of all sentient beings.

The broad outlines are:

I. Explaining the transmission in order to prove the authenticity of these instructions.

II. Explaining the exceptional qualities of this teaching in order to generate conviction in it.

III. The actual explanation of the practice.

I. EXPLAINING THE TRANSMISSION IN ORDER TO PROVE THE AUTHENTICITY OF THESE INSTRUCTIONS

I do not think it is necessary to trace the instructions back in detail, and in fact I do not remember all the historical facts related to the lineage. Actually its source is traced back to Buddha, who is the master of the doctrine. The compassionate and skillful Buddha taught many different teachings to suit the various dispositions and interests of the trainees. This guru yoga practice is a union of both sutra and tantra, so it explains the main theme of the *Prajnaparamita* sutras (which are the chief among the sutras). These sutras have two main aspects: the hidden meaning, which is the stages of the path, and the explicit meaning, which is emptiness. The two lineages known as the profound view and the vast practice, stemming from Manjushri and Maitreya respectively, evolved on the basis of these two aspects. The lineages of the tantric practices belong to the lineage of the experiential inspiration and those of lojong belong to the expansive deeds. These are the major lineages which originated in India.

Lama Tsongkhapa received all the transmissions which had come from India, of both the profound and the vast practices. There is an uncommon tradition coming from Lama Tsongkhapa, an ear-whispered transmission which has two lineages, one known as the lineage of Ensa and another called Segyue. As some scholars explain, one could also enumerate three major transmissions: Segyue, Ensa and Shungpa. The Segyue lineage, originating from the Tsang province, stems from Jetsun Sherab Senge, and the Shungpa, from central Tibet, also stems from Jetsun Sherab Senge. The Ensa lineage stems from the Khedup-je brothers.

Here is a brief explanation of the transmission of the short lineage. As written by Jamyang Choeje Tashi Paelden in the secret biography of Lama Tsongkhapa, the great lama had many visions of deities even as a child, and after he came to central Tibet, received many instructions and clarifications directly from Manjushri himself in the way of a disciple-teacher relationship. Then this transmission was handed down to Thogden Jampael Gyatso, who was a great being unparalleled in holding the lineage of the experiential inspiration of Tsongkhapa's doctrine. Then it went to Baso Choekyi Gyaltsen who had many disciples, the most widely known among them being the three Vajra brothers: Rinchen Dorje, one from eastern Tibet called Paelden Dorje, and Choekyi Dorje from Amdo. Each attained high realizations within his lifetime, achieving what is known as the rainbow body.

The mahasiddha Choekyi Dorje was born while his parents were on pilgrimage from Amdo. Baso Choekyi Gyaltsen saw that this small child was a very fortunate being of unusual faculties, so he looked after him and gave him all the profound instructions and transmissions. Choekyi Dorje achieved high realizations and finally the supreme enlightenment in his lifetime. He had all the transmissions coming from Lama Tsongkhapa, and it is said that he had a direct vision of him and received many different transmissions, in particular the instructions on the guru yoga practice of the triple being. His disciple was Ensapa, who achieved enlightenment within his lifetime, whose disciple was Khedup Senge Yeshe, whose disciple in turn was the author of this text, Panchen Lama Lozang Choekyi Gyaltsen. He lived a very long life and had great impact on the doctrine; he was a great being and non-sectarian, and his kindness to all Tibet was great.

Panchen Lama Choekyi Gyaltsen composed this guru yoga manual, and subsequently its transmission went to central Tibet and Amdo. Its use became very widespread during the lives of Panchen Paelden Yeshe, Puchog Ngawang Jhampa, Koenchog Jigme Wangpo and also Changkya Rolpai Dorje. Thus it also became very popular in the Amdo province. When the transmissions of this guru yoga practice and Panchen Lozang Choekyi Gyaltsen's text on mahamudra first came to Amdo, there was some initial apprehension, and the texts were closely scrutinized. I noticed this in one of the writings of Changkya Rolpai Dorje.

I received the transmission of the guru yoga from my root guru, the late Kyabje Trijang Rinpoche. The commentary I received was on the basis of Kachen Yeshe Gyaltsen's extensive commentary, and I also received the experiential commentary on the basis of the root text itself. There is another commentary which I hold very dear called *Kachem Lung Kurma* (Having Thrown to the Winds the Legacy of Oral Instruction) which has a reading transmission which I received as well.

In brief, the lineage of these instructions traces back to Buddha himself; in Tibet it started from Lama Tsongkhapa, and through Panchen Lozang Choekyi Gyaltsen it has come down to my root guru in an uninterrupted lineage.

II. EXPLAINING THE EXCEPTIONAL QUALITIES OF THIS TEACHING IN ORDER TO GENERATE CONVICTION IN IT

Now I will explain the greatness of this text. As I explained above, its source is traced to the root and explanatory tantras of Guhyasamaja. Therefore the great qualities of Guhyasamaja are also possessed by this instruction. Also, because all the instructions on the profound and vast practices are complete within this guru yoga, it has the qualities of the lamrim. Although all the teachings of sutra and tantra outline techniques for transforming one's state of mind, there is a specific set of teachings, called *lojong* or thought-transformation, in which great emphasis is placed on techniques for overcoming one's self-grasping and self-cherishing attitudes. It includes texts such as *Lojong Tsigyema* (Eight Verses on Thought Transformation). The great qualities of such instructions are also complete within the practice of this guru yoga.

The name of this text is *Guru Puja*, the method for offering to the guru. Although it was not necessary to give this text a Sanskrit name, as it is an indigenous Tibetan text, this was done in order to indicate its authenticity in being based on Indian works.

The verse of salutation reads:

> To the feet of the noble being, in dependence on whose
>   kindness
> the state of great bliss, the three bodies,
> and also the common powerful attainments
> can be achieved within an instant, I bow down.

Then comes the promise to compose the text:

> Having prostrated thus, I shall compose this text whose
> sources can be found in the root and explanatory tantras
> and also the commentaries by the Indian pundits, and
> which will be complemented by all the instructions of the
> gurus.

Then it reads:

> Such are the methods, for the fortunate who seek
> liberation.

The instructions of sutra and tantra are compared to a flower garden: Although this garden contains many varieties of flowers, one picks out the best ones and arranges a beautiful garland—"a well-arranged garland which could be worn with pleasure." This indicates that all the essential points of the sutras and tantras, which are like vast oceans, have been extracted and set down in a condensed form in this instruction.

Then the text goes on to say that the achievement of all excellences, including the two powerful achievements, is dependent on proper reliance on the guru, as explained in the Kadams' *Bhebum Ngonpo* (Blue Scripture), and in Lama Tsongkhapa's *Lamrim Nyamgurma* (Songs of Spiritual Experience). Also, as it says in the following verse from *Guru Panchasika* (The Fifty Verses of Guru Devotion):

> Having learned that Vajradhara said:
> "Powerful attainments depend on the guru,"
> Please the guru, your spiritual guide,
> With everything in your possession.

So, as stated here, as the person seeking enlightenment needs to engage in a path unknown to him, it is necessary to depend upon a proper guide who has great experience and qualifications. It is a fact that even an ordinary task which can be learned through observation requires guidance from an experienced person; in order to travel on the path to liberation and omniscience it is indispensable to rely upon an experienced and qualified master. Especially when one practices the path of tantra, it is necessary to take the guru yoga practice as the life of the path and cultivate resolute faith in one's guru. For these reasons, the successful practice of guru yoga constitutes making one's human life meaningful, thus taking the essence of one's precious human existence. Therefore, it is important to engage in such a practice.

III. THE ACTUAL EXPLANATION OF THE PRACTICE

The explanation of the actual text consists of:
   a) the preliminary activities
   b) the activities during the actual session, and
   c) the concluding activities.
These shall be discussed in detail later.

The Necessary Qualifications of the Practitioner
The basis for being able to undertake this guru yoga practice is that the practitioner should have received initiation into highest yoga tantra. Receiving initiation is not a simple thing. It has become a fashion these days to attend whenever someone is giving initiation. People think that just attending, even with a very distracted mind, even dozing off to sleep, is sufficient. That does not constitute having received the initiation. To receive initiation it is necessary to have had proper training in the common paths.   At least it is necessary to have an understanding of the general path as a whole. Although there are many different elements of the path, the most important are the three principal aspects—renunciation, bodhicitta and a correct view of emptiness. Generally speaking, it is necessary to have a genuine realization of these aspects. This may be difficult; one should at least have understanding of, or heartfelt admiration for, them. It is also necessary to have received the commentary of this instruction.

The Environment
For a hermit it is another matter, but for us "the environment" refers to our own rooms or houses or whatever. We have to remain in our homes irrespective of whether they are noisy or quiet and so on. When you are habituated to the practice and your mind is under control, external factors will not disturb you much, but at the beginners' level, external factors do interfere. For a beginner, it is recommended to undertake one's practice in a suitable place as explained in other texts— a good place, isolated, quiet, which has been blessed by noble persons. Most importantly, it should not have been a scene of battle or a place where a schism within a sangha community has occurred. So, in brief, you should try your best to make the place where you are staying as ideal an environment as possible.

The Actual Mode of Practice
There are many different modes of undertaking one's practice. Having chosen an ideal place, you should gather the articles necessary for the practice. If you have a representation of the merit field, like a thanka or a picture, it is very good. Or, it is also good to have a statue or photograph of Buddha or Lama Tsongkhapa or one's own root guru. If you do not have such things it will not matter much; you should not put too much emphasis on external articles like statues and so forth, but rather put more emphasis on your own inner realizations. Statues do help in explaining to beginners that such and such is the Buddha, such and such is Avalokiteshvara and so forth. Especially in countries like Tibet, where profound aspects of the dharma cannot be introduced these days, it is good to have statues of those beings in whom the person has great faith. Then one may at least be able to point the images out to a child, and say, for example, "This is the teacher, the Buddha; this is Manjushri—if you pray to him it will help your intelligence increase." But for a real practitioner, it is not necessary to depend upon these external factors, because the whole significance or purpose of practicing dharma is to perfect a

transformation in one's own mind. If a practitioner goes the other way, putting much emphasis on external factors like the material of statues, he might eventually start to regard them as possessions.

If you have statues, you should not discriminate between them on the basis of their materials, and you must arrange them in a proper order. Even if a statue of a buddha is made of clay, it has to be placed on a high level; and even if your statues of dharmapalas such as Mahakala are made of copper or brass or even solid gold they should be placed below. The proper order should be maintained. Especially, you should not have the attitude of their being your possessions. Although there are statues that were once owned by great beings and so forth, and that might have special power or sacredness, irrespective of their age or sacredness they have to be placed in the proper order. The whole purpose of regarding them as sacred is that they are to remind us of the actual deity or being that they represent. It is not the statue or the picture that we hold dear and venerate, rather it is what it represents. When we buy images of the Lord Buddha, it is to generate faith, because when we see them we recall his great kindness and qualities. Therefore, you should not discriminate between the statues according to the value of the material they are made from. The value of a statue is not less because it is made in Delhi!

It is necessary to have a text. If you are a lamrim practitioner, it is a must to have the long or short version of Lama Tsongkhapa's *Lamrim*. It would also be good if that could be complemented with texts such as *Ratnavali* (The Precious Garland) of Nagarjuna and also the *Bodhisattvacharyavatara* (Guide to the Bodhisattva's Way of Life). For a Gelug practitioner, *Lamrim Chenmo*, the long version of lamrim, is like the constitution! There are also important texts like *Drange Namje Lekshe Nyingpo* (The Discrimination of the Definitive and Interpretive Words of the Buddha) and the commentaries composed by Lama Tsongkhapa on *Madhyamaka-mulakarika* (the root text on wisdom by Nagarjuna) and *Madhyamakavatara*

(Chandrakirti's supplement). It is also good to have Panchen Lama Lozang Choekyi Gyaltsen's text on *choed*, cutting through the self-grasping attitude. Then, you can also arrange texts on lojong or other practices appropriately. Also, as a representation of the omniscient mind of the Buddha, it is good to have a stupa. Since you are a practitioner of highest yoga tantra, it is good to have religious articles such as vajra and bell and so forth; but if you do not practice properly but ring the bell very loudly and violently it does not help much! If you keep these religious objects on the basis of a good practice it is very good. Generally our attitude should be of putting more emphasis on the important things and less on the less important. If one were forced to choose, the choice should definitely be for the more important things. For instance, Gelugpas should regard the works of Lama Tsongkhapa as foremost and texts such as the text books of their own monastic universities as secondary. It is important to hold on to the root itself rather than onto the branches alone.

Generally it is said that when one undertakes a dharma meditation, one has to face towards the east, but this is not very important. It is good to have a seat with the rear slightly raised. For Westerners it may be difficult to sit in a cross-legged position. If you insist on it and exert yourself trying to do it, you might expend all your energy in sitting cross-legged, and there is a danger of all your mental energy going to your knees! Therefore, you can sit on a chair.

Since the accumulation of merit through the mandala offering is very important, it is good if you have a mandala. If you can afford it, it is good to have one made of gold or silver, but such things should not be viewed as possessions. If the material from which such articles are made is important, then such meditators as the mahasiddhas and Milarepa would not have achieved any realizations at all because they were poor, just like beggars. It is explained in *Chatu-Shataka Shastra* (Four Hundred Verses on the Middle Way) by Aryadeva that the practice of buddhadharma has to be undertaken on the basis of the mind, and therefore the external things are not important; it is the mind which matters.

2 *Preliminaries*

The preliminary activities consist of:
I. general preliminary practices, and
II. uncommon preliminary practices.

I. GENERAL PRELIMINARY PRACTICES

Regarding your daily practice, when you first wake up you should cultivate a very good motivation, thinking: I shall not spend this day in vain, but rather in a virtuous way. Reflect on the fact that you believe in something called dharma and have heard of, and believe in, the law of cause and effect, the theory of emptiness, love, compassion and so forth. So, being aware of all these factors, it is stupid to remain careless and unmotivated. For people like the Chinese communists who do not believe in such facts, it is a different matter; but for us who are aware of all these facts and have strong faith and belief in dharma, it would be stupid and sad if we were to spend our lives idly.

So, when you wake up, cultivate a proper motivation, thinking how best to spend that day; and at the end of the day you should review what kinds of activities you engaged in, and compare them with those of the previous day. This will help a lot.

When you see that you have erred and not practiced properly, you should regret it. The next morning you should reaffirm your resolve to right yourself and not waste your day, which has to be done through consciously bringing about some transformation in your attitudes. You should cultivate more determination within yourself through such a process. Your determination should be: Even if I may not be able to attain high realizations, at least I will not harm myself. The reason for not wasting even one day is that although the dharma is precious and effective, that in itself is not sufficient; one has to derive those benefits through practice.

Such practice can be done when one has obtained a suitable human form. We have to reflect on and rejoice in the fortune of having not taken rebirth in lower realms or as a human being in a country which is non-conducive for practicing dharma; also in having taken rebirth in a proper human form without any defects of the senses. All the main conditions for practicing dharma are complete, such as the external factor of actually having the presence of buddhadharma in the world, and also our having the necessary ability as a human being.

Reflecting on such facts, you should engage in the lamrim practices, cultivating the realizations of the three principal aspects of the path and the two stages of tantra. In order to make such practices more powerful and effective, it is necessary to recite mantras and so forth. There are certain practices such as blessing the speech which might help reduce the negativities accumulated through indulging in meaningless gossip and so on. You will find these in the manuals which outline the daily practices. It is necessary to make each and every day of our lives meaningful.

When you start your practice you should do so with the six preparatory practices.

1. Your environment, the room or house, should be clean. The motivation for cleaning your room should not be influenced by worldly attitudes; rather, you should think that because you are inviting the merit field, it is necessary to have the environ-

ment clean and tidy. If engaging in dharma practice becomes a non-virtuous action it is very sad. The impure aspects of the environment which we see are actually the products of our untamed mind. Therefore, if there is dust around and you do not desire such an unpleasant environment, you should search for the root cause. But I think it is necessary to clean the environment, especially in a place like Bodh Gaya where there is almost a hundred percent guarantee of catching a cold! But when we sweep the dust it causes us to cough and we do not like it, so we should search for the actual cause, and while we do the sweeping we should have the attitude: In fact I am cleaning my own ignorant mind. The more pleasant your environment is, the better it is for clarity of mind, which in turn will help your dharma practice.

2. Having thus cleaned the place, arrange the representations of the body, speech and mind of buddha, such as statues, scriptures and so forth, in the proper order. Then arrange representations of the deities as in the paintings. If you have a painting such as that of the merit field of *Lama Choepa*, it should not be hung too high, otherwise when you look at it to help you with your visualization, you may not be able to see the individual figures, and this might cause distraction.

3. Your offerings should not be influenced by fluctuations of motivation and they should not be procured by devious means—offerings procured through wrong means are not good offerings. They should be arranged with proper motivation. Just as explained in the precepts of refuge, you should make offerings of the first portion of your food or drink of the day, whether it be food, milk or tea. Offerings should be made of what is edible; it is not helpful to arrange a torma that could not be eaten and then to say OM AH HUM, OM AH HUM. If you can in reality transform something into delicious food just by reciting OM AH HUM three times, then it is alright! On the other hand, if your offerings remain as mere *tsampa* (roasted barley flour) after having repeated OM AH HUM a thousand times, it will not help much. The offerings should

be the best you can afford. At least you can offer the first portion of your daily food, as no one can live without food! Our offerings should be something which is edible.

After the Chinese invasion in the 1960s, the situation in Tibet was such that people had to eat mice, rats and so forth. People even said that a certain type of worm that looks a little oily really tasted very good! Some people told me that at the end of the day, when the evening course of indoctrination was over and they were finally given time to sleep, they went to the toilets and searched for certain worms which they collected and burnt in cigarette boxes and ate. It seems some people even had to eat human wastes. It is really very tragic! Those are exceptions—those types of edibles should not be offered! Canned food will not become dirty, and also it is edible. If you make water offerings in a proper manner, you can generate great merit.

4. Then, on a comfortable seat, you should sit in a position possessing the seven features[12] of the Vairochana posture. If crossing your legs is not comfortable, place them in a way that is. You can sit on a chair and say that you are following the example of Maitreya! Your hands should be placed at the level of your navel in the meditative equipoise posture, that is, the left palm below and the right palm above, the two thumbs touching, forming a triangular shape. Your spine should be straight as an arrow. The teeth and the lips should be left in the normal position and your tongue should touch the upper palate of your mouth so that you will not have saliva coming out during the meditation. It is said that when the upward moving wind becomes powerful it causes one to become thirsty, so if you keep your tongue touching the upper palate it will help this.

Your head should be slightly bent, your eyes directed at the tip of the nose. This does not mean that you should actually look at the tip of the nose—but if your nose is very long that would not be very difficult! But if your nose is very small your eyeballs will start aching! Europeans have very long noses, which is very convenient! If your eyes are downcast too much it will cause pain, so they should be kept in a normal position. At the beginning, closing your eyes might seem to help the clarity of visualization, but when you concentrate more deeply it will not help much. If you become habituated to your eyes being closed, there is actually more danger of mental sinking. On the other hand, if you train yourself in a meditational position with eyes open, although at the beginning things coming into your sight might disturb you, later it will help you have a very clear visualization. It seems that for someone who normally wears glasses, the visualization becomes clearer when he puts them on and can cause too much intensity, while taking them off can cause laxity! So, you should not purposefully close the eyes, but rather they should be kept in a natural position. After a while you will notice that you forget whether your eyes are open or closed.

Keep your shoulders in a natural position. If we add the appropriate breathing to these seven features it becomes the eight-fold posture of Vairochana.

5. Then check your mind for the presence of any strong emotion such as hatred or strong attachment towards any objects such as your possessions. For example, if you have very strong anger it has to be countered by meditating on love, especially focusing on that object of anger. You should transform the emotion through mental effort; or, instead of using a mental technique, you could concentrate on the movement of the wind. If you find your mind is very scattered, distracted, to calm it and to forget such distractions you should force all of your concentration onto the inhalation and exhalation of the breath, being aware of its process of movement: now it is going out, now it is coming in, I am inhaling, and so forth. This practice has to be done in a very gentle way. I have seen it explained in certain commentaries that when one has a negative mind of strong force such as anger, one should inhale and exhale more forcefully so that one can overcome the violent forces of the emotion. Because of the force of those minds themselves,

when one exhales violently and imagines that one is banishing the emotions, it seems one is helped a great deal. If you are doing this breathing process just for overcoming distractions, you should do it in a more gentle way, mentally counting the inhalations and exhalations: This is the first round...the second...and so on.

In the practice of the six yogas of Naropa, a process called "dispelling the impure winds through the nine rounds of breathing" is explained: First one inhales through the right nostril and exhales through the left, then one inhales through the left, and exhales through the right. In the auxiliary completion stage practice in the Vajrayogini sadhana, because of a special significance, the practice must be started with the left nostril. But when you do it on the basis of the six yogas of Naropa, first close the left nostril with the back of your right index finger and inhale through the right nostril, and then exhale from the left nostril while blocking the right nostril; after that, block the right nostril with your left index finger and so forth. During this process, although in reality you are inhaling and exhaling through the nostrils, imagine that the winds come out and go in through the two side channels. One can also do the practice without blocking the nostrils by hand. This will calm the force of whatever emotion you have, because it prevents reinforcement of it. The strong force of emotion calming down is just like turbid water becoming clear. A non-virtuous state of mind should be transformed to a neutral one and then skillfully transformed into a virtuous state.

6. Having accumulated the necessary articles, whether you are practicing properly or not depends only on your motivation. Therefore, as explained above, you should cultivate the motivation in the morning that you will make the most effective use of this day. You must develop the determination to make this day meaningful, because this precious human form is meaningful with respect to its potential. It is difficult to integrate your mind with virtue all the time, but think: While I am undertaking this practice of guru yoga, I must integrate

my mind with the dharma without being influenced by worldly attitudes. You must direct all of your concentration during the short duration of the session. The stronger your concentration is, the more meaningful your practice will be, and the more essence you can take of having obtained a human form. Reflect on topics such as the rarity of the precious human form, impermanence, death and so forth, and develop the determination: While I am doing this practice I will do it as well as possible; I shall not waste this life, and particularly this year, this month, this day and this very hour! When you take teachings from the Dalai Lama it should not be done deceptively—coming to the teachings with great enthusiasm, but not doing any practice when you return to your room. From one point of view, receiving the teachings and pretending that you are very interested is like deceiving the guru. The purpose of taking such teachings is to put them subsequently into practice. If you come to see some kind of spectacle, then I am just an actor, in which case after having seen the show you can just forget the whole thing; but this is not the case.

Over a period of days, months and years you can bring about an actual transformation of the mind, because it is the nature of the mind that it adapts to what is familiar. Consciousness does not have form, therefore it has no resistance to obstruction and it follows what is familiar and habitual. Although emotional afflictions do not have any form, they are very powerful because of our long habituation to them. Although we are aware of their defects and faults, we still fall under their influence because of our habituation. If you constantly familiarize yourself with your practice, you can definitely effect some change.

You may notice some difference between your present state of mind and that of ten years ago. Although it is very difficult for me to explain to others the importance of bringing about a transformation of the mind, since I myself have not been able to realize such a feat, yet if I compare my state of mind now with that of ten or twenty years ago, I see there has been a certain change in my understanding of emptiness, my experience of bodhicitta and so forth. At least I know the direction where bodhicitta lies! These experiences come about only through practice; they are not something that spontaneously arises. So, due to familiarity gained from training over the years, I think I see a certain difference, some effect in my mind—and I am not boasting about my realizations! The Dalai Lama was not born with the power to fly; if such was the case then it would not be encouraging—on the contrary, it might be discouraging.

Although, in order for people to develop faith, we say the Buddha has all the attributes and qualities, if you were urged to emulate him you might feel discouraged and reluctant, thinking: Oh, how can I ever achieve that? But you can take the example of lower beings such as the bodhisattvas on the path of meditation, the path of seeing, the path of preparation, and so forth. Especially, if you take as an example the bodhisattvas of the first path, the path of accumulation, you will have more courage and be able to emulate them. It is like when someone is in a race and his opponent is far ahead—he loses courage and hope. But, on the other hand, even if he is very tired, if he finds someone running alongside him he will gain courage and think: If I make a last attempt I might overtake him, and will again have hope of winning. In the same way, we should take the example of the members of the sangha community and try to emulate them and develop more courage.

In the past, the general style of teaching was that the gurus out of modesty always said that they themselves lacked the realizations but urged others to generate them. To modern audiences, such a style might seem discouraging. On the other hand, if the gurus say that they themselves have had some experience through meditation, and if that method is explained, this can help the listeners have more courage and inspiration; they will think: If I also undertake the practices I might get the same results.

It is only because of our lack of practice that we have remained in the same state. If we practice we can bring about a change. So, your practice should not be like deceiving the Dalai Lama! There are others more honest, who come to the teachings but do not have much interest: they doze off to sleep! They may come to the session having been so busy that they did not have time to rest well, and feel rested and warm and comfortable in the teaching hall! If you take teachings with a pure motivation, then you are seeking some kind of benefit for yourself; that benefit can only be brought about through practice. The best type of practice is to resort to solitude, being a hermit; that is very good, but it is also difficult. Moreover, if all of us become hermits we would die of starvation!

So, you must have the attitude: I must try my best during the short time that I engage in this practice of *Lama Choepa*, be it for one hour or two; I must make it most meaningful. Reflect on the significance of having obtained this precious human form. One hears many cases where people like ourselves, who have obtained a human form, die. This shows that our lives end. We see that when a person dies his belongings and his relatives and so forth are left behind, as there is no way that he can take them along with him. When we die, we have to leave even our own body behind; whether it is cremated, thrown in the water or electrically cremated, eventually no trace of it remains. There is also no way that you can take your friends; and there is no way you can have your guru actually go along with you. While you are alive, there may be others who have the strong wish and strong will to give their lives for you—for example, some say they would give their lives for the sake of the Dalai Lama. There are instances where people say to me, "I can give up my life for you"—but when such a situation arises they may back down! There would be some who could actually sacrifice their lives for my sake, but even so, when I die it will not help. But if I have engaged in a practice during my life in which I have used the force of my mind to transform it, that will help. We can see for a fact that things like relatives or belongings cannot help at that time.

One can never be sure when the phenomenon called death will come; nobody can have the certainty of how long he or she will live. Up to now we have depended on external factors like food, clothes, shelter and so forth to sustain our lives, but if we were to probe in detail we would know that there is no certainty regarding how long we are going to last. So think: If I were to die today, have I done enough practice? If you have practiced well and have purified your negativities and have had indications of a fortunate future through dreams and so forth, it is good; then you will not have regret at all. But if you were to die today without having done enough practice to bring about favorable consequences, then it is important to check if there is such a thing as rebirth or not. If there is no rebirth, then it is fine. Many do not accept rebirth because they have not understood it, but it is not that they have disproved its existence. If one holds the position that there is no rebirth, there are a lot of inconsistencies which cannot be explained. In buddhism, it is the general mode of approach that if a phenomenon is something beyond the perception of our direct experience, then it has to be inferred or proved through logical reasoning. If the phenomenon has more evidence to support it, and less or no evidence refuting its existence, then one should assume its existence. Because the phenomenon of rebirth has more reasons supporting it, if one holds to the opposite position, that there is no rebirth, there are a lot of contradictions. Apart from saying that we do not see or recall our past lives, we have no factual proof that they did not happen. Also, there are cases where people remember their past lives; this is not just a thing of the past, it happens even now.

Future lives are confined to two categories: favorable rebirths and unfavorable rebirths. The realms of hell and that of the hungry ghosts are not visible to us, but we can see animals being born, living and then dying. We can see that animals have strong emotional afflictions. Just as our own happiness and suffering are caused by our own past actions, in the same way the happiness and suffering of the animals are also caused by their past actions. We know that if we accumulate negative actions we will take rebirth as animals and so forth. Reflect upon such a fact and imagine what a fate that would be if you were to take rebirth as an animal! At present, we have obtained a precious human form and we also fight for human rights and so forth, but what would it be like if you were to die tomorrow and conceive inside a female dog? Even though we have obtained a favorable life as a human, we are still afflicted with lots of suffering and always plagued by dissatisfaction, discomfort and so forth; so how can we bear to envision such a fate?

If it is beyond your ability it is one thing, but if it is within your ability, you should develop the determination: I shall do my best. If you engage in this guru yoga practice with such an attitude, your progress will be very great, because through this practice you can leave an imprint on your mind for the realization of the entire path. Think: Having received an initiation and commentary, and instructions and blessings and so forth from my kind gurus, as an offering of realization to them I shall undertake this practice today to the best of my ability.

Such a virtuous mental attitude should not be influenced by selfish thoughts, but rather you should be more concerned with the welfare of other sentient beings. So, as it says in the manual, the preliminary practices such as taking refuge, the cultivation of the virtuous mind and the four immeasurables should be undertaken.

Refuge is what distinguishes a right path from a wrong path, and the generation of the bodhicitta is what distinguishes the mahayana from a lower path. These two factors are the essence of the entire dharma.

Refuge

In order to take refuge you should first visualize the object of refuge. However, you can take refuge without actually visualizing the object of refuge, but rather by reflecting on the qualities of buddha, dharma and the sangha. From among the Three Jewels, the understanding of the dharma is the most important. What is meant by *sangha* is a being who has had the first direct realization of the dharma at the learners' stage; a being who has a realization of dharma to the highest degree is a buddha. Reflect on the qualities of the dharma. You should go for refuge to these Three Jewels from the depth of your heart. Sometimes it is even better not to actually visualize the objects, else you might have the idea that when you invite the buddhas they appear, and otherwise they are not there. You can also take refuge—again without the visualization—by contemplating the qualities of the buddhas of the ten directions and their sons. But if you do visualize the objects of refuge as explained here, then you can perform the visualizations of nectar descending from them—a nectar which purifies your negativities and infuses you with inspiring strength.

One process of visualizing the object of refuge is known as *Kyatue Norbu Lug* (Jewel Tradition of Embodiment); a second method is called *Lama Denga* (Five Groups of Gurus), as described in the lamrim *Jorchoe* practice composed by the Third Dalai Lama. This is ideal for visualizing the object of refuge and for the generation of bodhicitta in general. A third tradition is as found here in *Lama Choepa*, which is quite similar to the Five Groups, and is the one described below.

The object of refuge is visualized thus: Above, in the space in front of you, at a distance such that if you were to make a prostration you would be able to reach it with the tips of your fingers, is a very expansive throne upraised by eight lions. In the center and in the four cardinal directions visualize five smaller thrones. On the central throne, which is slightly larger, visualize the master of the doctrine, Buddha Shakyamuni. Your mental image of the Buddha should not be like a statue, but rather, alive and radiant. On the Buddha's right is Maitreya; on his left, Manjushri. Maitreya is surrounded by the lineage gurus of the vast practices, starting from Asanga, and Manjushri is surrounded by the lineage gurus of the profound view, starting from Nagarjuna. Behind Buddha, visualize Vajradhara surrounded by the lineage gurus of the experience lineage. The term *experience lineage* has many connotations; here take the lineage of the meditational deity that you mainly practice.

In front, in the center visualize your own root guru, who

is kind in three ways and in whom you have the strongest faith. Actually, during guru devotion practices one should not have any partial feelings towards one's gurus, but rather, one should see them all as actual buddhas, beginning with the teacher who first taught one the alphabet. But for a beginner who has yet to develop such an attitude, it is helpful to focus more on a single guru, the one with whom one feels more affinity and stronger faith, and then later direct the correct feeling onto the others. Visualize that guru in front in his normal form, but if he has any defects of his eyes and so on they should not be visualized. Otherwise, he should be visualized in his normal appearance. He is surrounded by the other gurus from whom one has received teachings, all of them facing towards oneself. So, altogether there are five groups of gurus.

Visualize the meditational deities of the four classes of tantra, ranged in circles around the five groups of gurus. In the innermost circle are the deities of highest yoga tantra: next are those of yoga tantra, then of performance tantra and then of action tantra. Outside the meditational deities are buddhas, bodhisattvas, heroes, dakinis, etc.

You yourself are surrounded by all the sentient beings of the six realms. As explained by Gungtang Rinpoche, it is auspicious to visualize all of them in the forms of human beings because these are appropriate forms for gaining realizations. But you can also visualize them in their individual forms so that you can generate stronger compassion focused on their suffering fate. I think you could first visualize them in their individual forms and later, when you do the visualization of nectars descending and purifying the negativities, visualize them being transformed into the aspect of human beings. As the masters of the past said, "Objects of refuge pervade space while sentient beings cover the ground." When you go for refuge, imagine yourself being like the *umdze*, the leading chanter, while reciting the refuge formula.

What is meant by going for refuge is that you are seeking refuge from some fear. All the objects in front of you are what is known as the causal refuge, because they serve as the cause

for bringing about the resultant refuge within you. You should
entrust yourself to these objects from the depth of your heart,
and you should see the objects as protectors. The resultant state
of your own future realizations, becoming an Arya being and
attaining buddhahood—which depends on your own actualization of the path—is called the resultant refuge. Someone in
difficulty seeking the assistance of a high official is analogous
to someone seeking refuge in the causal refuge. But depend-
ing upon others' protection forever is not a courageous way
of life; therefore, one has to try to achieve a state where one
is no longer dependent upon such a refuge, and this is likened
to taking refuge in the resultant buddha, dharma and sangha.
That is the process of taking refuge by a person of high faculty
and courage. This practice should be done not for the sake
of oneself alone but rather for the sake of all other sentient
beings. When you cultivate such an aspiration focused towards
the achievement of the omniscient state, it is very much like
the generation of the bodhicitta mind. A mahayanist[13] is more
courageous and also has higher faculties.

In order to have a proper practice of refuge, you should think
about the reasons for going for refuge to such objects. Here
you should reflect upon the causes of refuge. If you are free
of all fears and sufferings, then you do not have to go for refuge to someone; but since that is not the case, you have to
take refuge in someone who has achieved a state free from
suffering. Therefore, it is necessary to reflect on the general
and specific sufferings of cyclic existence and to understand
that the Three Jewels possess the ability to rescue you from
such dangers. This does not apply to you alone, but is the same
for all other sentient beings as well. Contemplate the suffering of oneself and other sentient beings: how we are afflicted
at the present, and have the potential for being afflicted by
sufferings in the future as well. The causes for future suffering that we have within ourselves are like the treasure stores
of the kings. If there is no release from such suffering and
fear, it is one thing, but such is not the case. So we have to
seek the means by which we can be free of them. Such free-

dom can be achieved by actualizing the cessations, which requires the practice of the truth of the path. For this it is necessary to seek the protection of the Buddha who can show us the proper path. Also, we need a sangha community as companions. And we need the guru to actually guide us on the path.

Of these three objects of refuge, the most important is the dharma, which consists of the cessations, and the realizations of the path leading to them. It is the dharma which actually protects us from the fears; for instance, the cessations within the mental continuum of the Buddha protect him from all fears. Thus it is necessary to have a very good understanding of what is called the dharma. For this, I think, it is necessary to have a very good understanding of the four noble truths. This in turn requires an understanding of the two truths, without which it is difficult to generate strong conviction in the four noble truths. Therefore Buddha gave all his teachings on the basis of, or in dependence on, the two truths. If your faith is based on an understanding of the four noble truths, or the two truths, you will have a very strong belief in the infallibility of the objects of refuge; you will be able to recognize the fear and also cultivate the strong conviction that such objects of refuge have the ability to protect you from this fear.

So, if we seek refuge in a being like the Buddha who has actualized such a state, he is able to show us the path through which he had his own experience. The buddhas in front of you have actualized what is called the truth of the path, the realizations, and have eliminated all the objects of negation and achieved cessation; such a state is possible and existent as an object of knowledge. You can see the possibility of such a state through the reasonings[14] employed for proving yogic direct perception. Hence you will understand that the buddhas in front of you are existent now and are not mere historical figures, and that others have the capacity to realize such a state. It is beyond question that we desire happiness and do not want suffering, so we have to actualize what is called the truth of the path in order to achieve that. Therefore, it is necessary to have a guide, a guru, who can show the right path. And we need a sangha community as companions on the path. Thus you can realize that the Three Jewels as objects of refuge are indispensable and also that they are undeceiving when refuge is sought in them.

With such reflections, go for refuge to the buddha, dharma and sangha, entrusting yourself from the depths of your heart. The ultimate purpose of doing so is to cultivate the realizations which bring about the cessations of delusions and their imprints within your own and other sentient beings' mental continuums. Thus, regard the Buddha as the guide who leads us on the path; the dharma as the actual path; and the sangha as noble companions on the path. On the basis of such a strong feeling of trust, recite the refuge formulas either together—"I go for refuge to the Buddha, dharma and sangha"—or individually. In addition to the Three Jewels, another object of refuge is the guru. In reality there is no separate guru; the guru is actually included in either Buddha or sangha, but because it is the guru who introduces us to, and brings about the inspiration and blessings of, the Three Jewels within our minds, we take specific refuge in the guru first.

You should not regard the guru as someone superior to the Buddha. I have a friend, a Westerner, who told me that on a pilgrimage he went on, the people actually regarded gurus as superior to Lord Buddha himself. He said he did not like it, and I feel he was right. If one's attitude towards the Buddha is of his being inferior to one's own guru, it is not very good. Because guru yoga is so much emphasized in Tibetan buddhism, some people misunderstand, thinking that Tibetans have four objects of refuge, one extra, and therefore think it is appropriate to call Tibetan buddhism *lamaism*!

The guru is a person with whom we can have intimate contact and with whom we have a teacher-disciple relationship. It is only through our guru that we can receive teachings and instructions. Lord Buddha himself is such a superior being; as far as we are concerned he is only an object of aspiration and prayer. We can go to the sacred places like Bodh Gaya and

Kushinigar and pray to him, but that is all we can do, although there could be a few exceptions where someone could have actual contact. Therefore, the being most kind to us is the guru. It is said:

> If you understand, not just in mere words,
> The way in which buddhas and bodhisattvas of the past
> help the beings of the present age,
> It comes down to the qualified gurus.

This verse is very powerful.

So you should entrust yourself to these four objects of refuge from the depth of the heart, not just with mere words alone, and thus repeat the formula. In the formula for taking refuge in the Three Jewels which we normally recite, the line regarding the guru is very effective and powerful.

When you take refuge in the guru, focus your concentration chiefly on your root guru, but also on the other gurus from whom you have taken teachings. Then recite the formula, "I go for refuge to the guru (*namo gurubhyah*)," until there is some effect in your mind. Your practice of refuge should not be judged by the number of recitations you make! Imagine that all sentient beings have the same type of attitude and strong force of mind and are also reciting the same formula in unison. Make fervent prayers from the depth of your heart, and imagine nectars pouring down from the gurus, particularly from your root guru, entering your body and the bodies of sentient beings. Imagine that the nectars sort of slide down the light rays that emanate from the guru's body. They purify all the negativities committed throughout past lives, especially the negativities of having disturbed the minds of the gurus, and the negativities committed in relation to the bodies, speech and minds of the gurus, and to having been divisive or having insulted gurus. All of these without exception are purified, and they emerge from the bodies of yourself and all sentient beings in the aspect of black, inky liquids. Imagine that all the negativities are purified, and think that we are all placed under the care of the venerable guru and that we receive inspiration and blessings.

Next, recite the formula for taking refuge in the Buddha, using the same type of visualization. When you do the recitation of going for refuge to the dharma, you should focus on the actual dharma, the cessations and realizations, visualized in the form of scriptures in front of each merit field figure. You should imagine nectars following from these scriptures and do the visualizations of purification.

During all these visualizations of taking refuge, imagine the negativities being purified and especially the negativities committed in relation to the relevant object of refuge. Take, for example, dharma: the negativities of abandoning dharma, putting texts on mattresses or walking over them and so forth, and the negativities committed by those who make profit from selling texts and statues and so forth. There are a lot of negativities committed in relation to dharma. When we live in the sangha community, we create a lot of negativities especially in relation to the sangha. Sometimes we insult or speak against someone and so on. Gungtang Rinpoche said that all the happiness of sentient beings, including human beings and gods, depends on the doctrine, the survival of which depends on the sangha community. Therefore, if someone misappropriates the possessions of the sangha community, it is a great negativity. Imagine that all the negativities or shortfalls that might have been committed in relation to the objects of refuge have been purified.

Take refuge in these four objects—guru, buddha, dharma and sangha—and recite the formula and do the visualization of nectars descending and so forth. Imagine that all the negativities of all the sentient beings surrounding you, especially those committed in connection with the three refuges and the gurus, come out of their bodies in the form of black liquids like inks and sink into the ground. Imagine that these negativities flow into the mouths of harmful spirits, satisfying them, or into the mouth of Yama who resides below the earth, and that he becomes satisfied. Through the force of the blessings of the Three Jewels and also your own force of prayer, the negativities actually become like nectar and satisfy them. It is said that once satisfied, their mouths should be sealed with a golden wheel. The significance of this visualization has to do with a practice for the prolongation of life. Imagine that you and all other sentient beings are placed under the care of these objects of refuge. Thus undertake the visualization of the three features of the refuge practice: purification, receiving the inspirations, and being placed under the care of the objects of refuge. That constitutes taking refuge. If you have time you should repeat this practice as much as possible, until there is some kind of impact on your mental continuum.

Generating the Altruistic Mind
Next is the generation of bodhicitta. Contemplate on the fact that all sentient beings who surround you have actually been your own mothers during innumerable lives. You can also reflect on the technique of exchanging yourself for others: All sentient beings as infinite as space are equal in that they do not desire suffering and do want happiness. Think that the happiness and fate of sentient beings infinite as space are really very important. Reflect upon the fact that all sentient beings have been kind to you in many ways. As explained in the *Bodhisattvacharyavatara*, there are many reasons for cultivating bodhicitta. Focus on those and generate compassion for sentient beings. Then, on the basis of compassion and love you should cultivate the actual bodhicitta. Also, remember that all the buddhas of the past have achieved enlightenment for the sake of all sentient beings and that their activities are aimed at bringing about the welfare of sentient beings; so, as a follower of Lord Buddha it is your duty to fulfill the wishes of these buddhas. Therefore think: On my part I should not abandon sentient beings; even if it is very small, I must make a contribution to the happiness of other sentient beings—even if it is just the verbal recitation of a prayer; therefore, I shall expend all the effort and ability that I have in order to provide happiness for all sentient beings; and unless I achieve the enlightened state, there is no way I can bring about their welfare.

Cultivate a bodhicitta induced by the unusual attitude and love and compassion. You could do that on the basis of reciting the verse "Sangye Choetsogma."[15] As the first two lines relate to refuge, you could repeat them many times when you take refuge. As you recite the next two lines, reflect upon the generation of bodhicitta. If you are doing this practice on the basis of this formula repeat it until there is some kind of effect in your mind.

Here you can undertake the practice of what is called "bodhicitta, taking the result into the path." Imagine that as you have engaged in the very worthwhile practices of taking refuge and cultivating the altruistic attitude of bodhicitta, the Buddha is very pleased, and nectars descend from him. A replica of Lord Buddha emerges and dissolves into you. Cultivate the bodhicitta and imagine that you arise into the Lord Buddha himself. Duplicates of the Lord Buddha, equal to the number of sentient beings, emerge from your body and dissolve into the sentient beings. Their negativities are purified and they become enlightened and arise into the Buddha's form. That is called "generation of the mind taking the result into the path." Because in reality we have not become enlightened, this practice is done only on the imaginary level. Then think: Although I have cultivated such a noble state of mind, it is only in my imagination; what is it that prevents the realization of such a state in reality? You will find that it is because your mind is gripped by emotions and biased attitudes towards others.

We have to undergo suffering even though we do not want it. We know that the cause of it is the force of our own emotional afflictions. In order to overcome these negative forces and balance our attitudes toward all beings, we should engage in the practice of the four immeasurables,[16] starting with equanimity. Each of the four immeasurables itself has four factors—the immeasurable wish, the immeasurable aspiration, the immeasurable attitude and the immeasurable prayer. Think: Although I have done this meditation, it is just on the level of imagination. The factor which prevents you actualizing such a state is the fluctuation of the emotional afflictions that you experience in relation to other sentient beings. Then cultivate immeasurable compassion and immeasurable equanimity and so forth, requesting the guru-deity to enable you to cultivate them within yourself. The practice of the four immeasurables is an impetus for the practice of bodhicitta.

From here on, the commentary will be based on the verses of the *Lama Choepa* text itself.

1. FROM WITHIN GREAT BLISS I MANIFEST AS A
       GURU-DEITY;
    FROM MY BODY A PROFUSION OF LIGHT RAYS
       RADIATE FORTH TO THE TEN DIRECTIONS
    TRANSFORMING THE ENVIRONMENT AND THE
       BEINGS THEREIN—
    ALL BECOMES MOST PERFECTLY ARRAYED
       WITH ONLY INFINITELY PURE QUALITIES.

In this text, the practices of self-generation and consecration of the environment come first. There is a tradition where these are performed later, but they can be done in this order too, because nobody should practice *Lama Choepa* who has not received a high tantric initiation. We visualized experiencing great bliss during the initiation and thus have been introduced to this wisdom of great bliss and emptiness. At this point, you should think about the experience of great bliss. When you wake up in the morning and are about to become alert after the intoxication of sleep, it is good if you can think that you are being awakened by songs of emptiness. Do you do that? You should, even if only at the imagination level, experience the clear light of sleep and from within that clear light arise as the deity. The process of arising into the deity in the morning should not be gradual like a crow chick turning black, but rather you should arise into the deity the moment you wake up. Although in reality you are an ordinary being, at least on the imagination level you can arise into the chief meditational deity you practice—that is, the action deity of that particular meditational deity. If, for example, you are practicing Yamantaka, you should arise into simple Yamantaka, one face and two arms. Also, cultivate the clarity of the visualization. Irrespective of whether you have been mindful of the deity or not in the morning, it is very good to arise as the deity at the beginning of the session. Therefore, it is also suitable to perform these practitices according to the order found in the text, which is the tradition of Khedup Sangye Yeshe.

The use of the words "manifest as a guru-deity" is to emphasize the importance of seeing the meditational deity as inseparable from the guru. Because guru yoga is like the life of the path, in order to underline its extreme importance Khedup Sangye Yeshe and Gyalwa Ensapa coined such terms as "Lama Lozang Thubwang Dorje Chang," "Guru Chakrasamvara," "Guru Akshobhya" and so forth. As Sangye Yeshe's guru was Ensapa Lozang Dhondrub, he even went to the extent of calling his meditational deities by the name of Lozang, like "Lozang Chakrasamvara," "Lozang Akshobhya" and so on.

At this point you can meditate on the three bodies. For that, first dissolve yourself into emptiness and meditate on emptiness. Contemplate, at least with effort, on the fact that all phenomena lack inherent nature. Imagine that your mind that reflects on emptiness is experiencing great bliss. On the basis of that, think that this is the truth body, and cultivate divine pride focused on that. Then, through the intention of arising into the enjoyment body, visualize a beam of light. Next, through the force of the intention to arise into an emanation body, imagine instantly arising into a simple Yamantaka, one face, two arms.

From the entire body of the deity, and in particular from the syllable HUM at the heart, light rays radiate in all the ten directions and purify the environment as well as the beings within it, transforming them into a manifestation of bliss and emptiness. Because we imagine that we generate blissful wisdom focused upon emptiness, and since all phenomena are manifestations of emptiness, through our imagination we can see that all phenomena are also manifestations of the great bliss that is conjoined with emptiness. That is how one consecrates the environment and the beings within it. So, the impure environments become pure celestial mansions and the beings within them pure, divine, male and female deities.

You can cultivate these attitudes as the first practice as soon as you awaken from sleep, then engage in other practices such as prostrations, circumambulations and so forth, and then do your everyday activities such as eating breakfast. If you do your sadhanas very early, do them after you have washed yourself. Although you have cultivated clarity of the visualization and divine pride of a deity, it is not contradictory to do the practices of refuge and so forth. Just as one does during the Vajrasattva meditation and recitation which is performed at the beginning of a sadhana, retain the divine appearance and the divine pride without emphasizing them during such practices.

2. FROM THE STATE OF AN EXALTED, WHITE VIRTUOUS MIND,
   I AND ALL THE INFINITE SENTIENT BEINGS,
   MY MOTHERS OF OLD,
   FROM THIS MOMENT UNTIL OUR SUPREME ENLIGHTENMENT
   GO FOR REFUGE TO THE GURUS AND THE THREE JEWELS.

3. NAMO GURUBHYAH,
   NAMO BUDDHAYA,
   NAMO DHARMAYA,
   NAMO SANGHAYA.

Here the appropriate motivation is bodhicitta, the altruistic attitude. You should cultivate such a mind, even if simulated, as strongly as possible.

Visualize objects of refuge as explained earlier, or you can visualize them as being the same as the merit field, leaving out the wish-granting tree and the ocean of milk. Then, having visualized them, from the depth of your heart you should reflect on fear, faith and conviction. Through the aggregation of these three factors, seek refuge with strong faith and then recite *Namo Gurubhyah* until there is some effect with in your mind. If you do not find the Sanskrit version very effective, you can say the phrase in Tibetan or your own language. But if it is just as easy for you, use the Sanskrit version as it has special power. So, make request-prayers to the objects of refuge and do the visualization of nectars descending and so forth as explained earlier.

4. FOR THE SAKE OF ALL MOTHER SENTIENT
   BEINGS
   I SHALL BECOME A GURU-DEITY,
   AND THUS PLACE ALL SENTIENT BEINGS
   INTO THE SUPREME STATE OF A GURU-DEITY.

This is the generation of bodhicitta. For the sake of all mother sentient beings, having become the guru-deity, I shall place them in the same state that I have actualized myself. The object of intent for the cultivation of bodhicitta is the innumerable sentient beings. One brings about the welfare of sentient beings by placing them in the state of buddhahood, and the way in which one can accomplish such welfare is by showing them the correct path. It is only a buddha who has the full capacity to bring about such welfare; therefore, for the sake of mother sentient beings, develop the motivation: I shall attain the state which has such a capacity.

5. FOR THE SAKE OF ALL MOTHER SENTIENT
   BEINGS
   I SHALL QUICKLY, QUICKLY, IN THIS VERY
   LIFE,
   ATTAIN THE STATE OF A PRIMORDIAL
   BUDDHA, GURU-DEITY.

6. I SHALL LIBERATE ALL MOTHER SENTIENT BE-
   INGS FROM SUFFERING

AND LEAD THEM TO THE GREAT BLISS OF
BUDDHAHOOD.
TO THIS END I NOW SHALL PRACTICE
THE PROFOUND PATH OF GURU-DEITY YOGA.

This is what is known as the special generation of the mind,
which cannot be cultivated by bodhisattvas of inferior courage. It pledges: I shall liberate all mother sentient beings from
suffering and lead them to the great bliss of buddhahood.
Think: For the sake of helping all sentient beings I shall achieve
the enlightened state—the union of illusory body and clear
light—in the shortest possible time, and for that purpose I am
going to engage in the practice of this guru yoga. The attitude
of wishing to bring about such welfare and to place sentient
beings in buddhahood is not just a relaxed state of mind, but
rather one of great urgency. It is a mind aspiring to achieve
enlightenment within one lifetime, and that within the shortest time possible. Regarding the words "quickly, quickly," the
first "quickly" refers to the period of twelve years, the second "quickly" refers to the shortest possible time, which is
three years.

The best kind of attitude is, having reflected on the fate of
sentient beings, to think: I cannot bear to see the suffering
of sentient beings even for one more moment. If such an anx-
ious mind is induced by this motivation, that is the best type
of attitude. On the other hand, if you think: I must achieve
buddhahood as quickly as possible so that I can enjoy a blissful state, your force of mind will not be very strong. Compared to the latter motivation, cultivating the determination
to achieve buddhahood for the sake of all sentient beings—
even if you might have to undergo practices for three incalculable eons, as in the sutra vehicle—from one point of view
appears more courageous. Bodhisattvas who accumulate merits
for the first incalculable eon during the paths of accumulation and preparation, for the second during the first bodhisattva
grounds and for the third during the last three grounds are
really very courageous. They have such strong determination

and resolve! Nagarjuna's *Ratnavali* explains how the bodhisattvas accumulate the merits necessary for the achievement
of the major and minor noble marks of a buddha, and how
even to achieve one hair of a pore of a buddha's body requires
great stores of merit. If you reflect on these facts you will find
them really inconceivable.

For example, your attitude should not be such that when
you start a long-term retreat it is with strong determination
and the expectation that you will be able to fly when you fin-
ish it, yet when you emerge at the end and do not see much
difference (and perhaps on the contrary find that as a result
of sitting for too long you even have to limp a bit!), you lose
hope and courage and think: Oh, there's no hope for me! That
kind of approach is wrong.

You should reflect on the necessity of accumulating merits
for incalculable eons. If doing so causes you to feel discouraged,
it is helpful to reflect on the fact that such an accumulation
can be achieved within a short period of time through tantric
practices. It is also helpful to contemplate on the buddha nature that is inherent within everyone, and also that the buddhas
are actively engaged in helping us. In buddhism, many techniques are taught, from many different perspectives, and these
should be incorporated into your practice. In order to tame
our rough minds, it is necessary to seek an approach through
all possible avenues. Here the generation of bodhicitta should
be very forceful, with a very courageous mind.

At this point you can also do the practice of what is called
"generation of the mind taking the result into the path." As
explained before, it is good to practice the uncommon or special preliminary practices in connection with Yamantaka by
doing the instantaneous self-generation of Yamantaka. There
are three ways to do the dissolution of the object of refuge as
found in practices for taking death into the path as the dharmakaya: absorbing it through your mid-brow and blessing yourself and then doing the self-generation; dissolving it by visualizing the beings departing to their natural abodes; and keeping
it as wisdom beings which can be dissolved into the merit field,

which is visualized later.

The explanations on refuge, on the generation of the bodhimind and on the four immeasurables are over. Up to this point we have covered the general preliminary practices, and what follows now are the uncommon preliminary practices.

II. UNCOMMON PRELIMINARY PRACTICES

Develop strong faith focused on the objects of refuge in front of you, which pleases them; through the force of their pleasure they dissolve into you; imagine that through the force of their dissolving you receive their blessings and inspirations within your mental continuum. Imagine that your body, speech and mind become inseparable and of one taste with the body, speech and mind of the guru, and due to that you experience great bliss. While in this state, meditate on emptiness. After that, dissolve into emptiness. It is explained that at this point one should do the meditation of taking death into the path as the truth body. You can do this according to the process known as the "dissolution process of entirety."[17] After that you can practice taking the intermediate state into the path as the enjoyment body by visualizing arising into a blue light beam, and then arise as Yamantaka according to the instantaneous self-generation, and generate the pride of being the emanation body. That is the shorter version of generating into the deity.

If you want to elaborate slightly, at this point arise as Yamantaka with a consort. From the syllable HUM at your heart, light rays radiate in all directions, transforming the environments into celestial mansions and the beings within them into Yamantakas. The celestial mansions dissolve into the Yamantakas which dissolve into you. Then imagine experiencing the various appearances associated with the dissolution of the elements: first, the mirage-like vision, the internal sign of the dissolution of the earth element, as the consort dissolves into you and you dissolve into the syllable HUM from above and below. Next comes the smoky vision, the sign of the water element dissolving, as the vowel U of the HUM dissolves into the body of the HA. Then, associated with the dissolution of the elements, a vision like fireflies arises as the HA dissolves into its top line. When the top line begins to dissolve into the crescent, the wind dissolves into appearance and you imagine experiencing a glow similar to that of a butter lamp. The dissolution of appearance is in turn divided into three: the white radiant, the red increase and black near-attainment. These correspond to the dissolution of the crescent, circle and nada. Then you experience the clear light; the appearance at this point is like a clear sky at dawn during autumn which is free of sun, moon and darkness. In this state even the three appearances are purified.

At this stage the appearance is of emptiness, but you should not leave the empty appearance as mere absence of phenomena, or a vacuum, but rather qualify it by the apprehension of emptiness of inherent existence. The consciousness which realizes that emptiness should be imagined as simultaneously blissful; on this basis, cultivate the divine pride of being the resultant truth body.

If you were to remain in meditative equipoise in that expanse of the truth body, you would not be able to fulfill your pledge of bringing about the welfare of other sentient beings. Therefore to fulfill this pledge that you made at the time of cultivating the bodhicitta, you arise as the form body, in this case as the deity Yamantaka, with one face and two arms, which is the enjoyment body. Generate the divine pride of being the enjoyment body.

If you were to remain in that state of the enjoyment body you would not be visible and directly accessible to ordinary beings. Therefore develop the attitude: In order to benefit ordinary beings I will arise into the emanation body. Arise as Yamantaka, and mark the three parts of your body with the syllables OM AH HUM. Placing these three syllables on the body of Yamantaka constitutes the arisal into the full emanation body. This has been explained in the *Kachem Lung Kurma* text.

The most elaborate way to arise into the deity is as found in the Yamantaka sadhana itself—the gradual process, first visualizing the mandala with the cemeteries and everything else, and then the actual deity. So, there are three ways of arising into the deity: the shortest, instantaneous generation; the middling, as described above; and the longest, as found in the sadhana. Regardless of the length, it is important to have complete the main points of taking the three bodies into the path. This could be done in connection with whichever meditational deity you practice by arising into that particular deity. The nature of the wisdom of bliss and emptiness first appears as a light beam, the form of the enjoyment body, and then you arise into the deity. Cultivate clarity and divine pride.

Consecration of the Offerings

7. OM AH HUM, OM AH HUM, OM AH HUM.

8. PURE CLOUDS OF OUTER, INNER AND SECRET OFFERINGS,
   AND RICH OFFERINGS OF RITUAL REQUIRE-MENTS SPREAD INCONCEIVABLY,
   PERVADING THE REACHES OF SPACE, EARTH AND SKY;
   IN ESSENCE THEY ARE PRISTINE AWARENESS, IN ASPECT INNER OFFERINGS AND THE VAR-IOUS OBJECTS OF OFFERING.
   THEIR FUNCTION AS OBJECTS TO BE ENJOYED BY THE SIX SENSES
   IS TO GENERATE THE EXTRAORDINARY PRIS-TINE AWARENESS OF VOIDNESS AND BLISS.

To perform the consecration of the offerings more elaborately, one can follow the Yamantaka sadhana: first the consecration of the inner offering and then the consecration of the other offerings. The shorter method is performed by visualizing the three syllables OM AH HUM in space above the offering substances. Light rays radiate from the syllables, invoking the blessings of vajra body, vajra speech and vajra mind—the deities of the three vajras: Vairochana, Amitabha and Akshobhya—which dissolve into the three syllables respectively. Imagine that the syllable HUM blesses the substances of offering, thus purifying their impure aspects such as bad odors, tastes and shape. The syllable AH transforms them into nectar. There are three types of nectar: the immortal nectar, the wisdom nectar and the uncontaminated nectar. The syllable OM—the seed-syllable of Vairochana—increases all the offerings: imagine that all these offerings become inexhaustible.

The offerings are endowed with three attributes, their nature being the wisdom of bliss and emptiness. For example, we can say that although by nature a certain Tibetan food called *baktsa marku* is made of flour, it has its own particular characteristics. By nature, bread is flour, but there are different types of bread: the appearance is bread, but it can be oily or without oil and so on. If, on the other hand, we talk of *momos*, there should be meat inside. Because they have different appearances they also have different flavors: *kapsey*, the Tibetan biscuit, has its own characteristic taste; and *timo*, the steamed *momo*, also has its own flavor. The shapes themselves are also offerings! They each have a pleasant flavor to offer the tongue. Likewise, these offering substances have different functions. For instance, forms induce bliss within the eye organ and the other offerings induce bliss in the other senses. If you can afford to do so you should actually set out these objects of offering, then purify, transform and increase them. Imagine them as being endowed with the three attributes: a nature of the wisdom of bliss and emptiness; an individual appearance; and a function to induce bliss within the senses of the object of offering. This concludes the instruction on the preliminary practices.

3 *Visualization of the Merit Field*

You have arisen into the deity using either the long or short version of the self-generation procedure. While in such a form, it is necessary to effect a transformation within your mind, as explained during the initiation in the section where one has to cultivate what is called the "mind of all-encompassing yoga." First develop at least an intellectual understanding of the wisdom of bliss and emptiness and generate that wisdom, even though it might be merely imaginary. It is good to read from the root text with such a state of mind, otherwise it will be just mere words. So, first cultivate the wisdom of bliss and emptiness. If you have generated yourself into both Yamantaka and consort, you should try to induce bliss by visualizing entering into union with the consort and experiencing the four joys, culminating in the fourth, the simultaneous joy, even though it might be on the imaginary level. Within that joy, meditate upon the non-inherent nature of phenomena. To do this you can employ many types of reasonings, such as the absence of singularity and plurality, or the "diamond sliver" reasoning[18] etc. Having employed these various types of reasonings, analyze the nature of phenomena: that the one who enjoys, lacks inherent existence, and the objects of enjoyment lack an inherent nature—but all of them exist in dependence on causal factors. Cultivate this ascertainment, the wisdom which is the indivisibility of bliss and emptiness, even though it might be simulated. It is good to recite the text on the basis of such reflections.

9. IN THE VAST SPACE OF INDIVISIBLE VOIDNESS AND BLISS,
   AMIDST BILLOWING CLOUDS OF SAMANTAB-HADRA OFFERINGS,
   AT THE CREST OF A WISH-GRANTING TREE EM-BELLISHED WITH LEAVES, FLOWERS AND FRUIT,
   IS A LION THRONE ABLAZE WITH PRECIOUS GEMS, ON WHICH IS A LOTUS, SUN AND FULL MOON.

In all the manuals on tantric practice, the wisdom of bliss and emptiness is referred to repeatedly. Here, in the section on the visualization of the merit field, the text speaks of an expansive space of bliss and emptiness: "space" here refers interpretively to literal space, and definitively to the wisdom of bliss and emptiness. In *Thundrug Lamai Naljor* (Six Session Guru Yoga) we find: "In the space in front, on a beautiful jewel throne...," and in the ritual manual of Paelden Lhamo it reads: "All phenomena that appear are the manifestation of the wisdom of bliss and emptiness." If one makes offerings, keeping this viewpoint in mind, it is good. It is from the expanse of reality, of this wisdom of indivisible bliss and emptiness, that the various emanations of both the learner and no-more-learning stages arise. Therefore, cultivate this wisdom, even if it is only in the imagination. The Seventh Dalai Lama, Kelsang Gyatso, also emphasized the point that all the offerings should be made within seeing them as the manifestation of the wisdom of bliss and emptiness. To quote from one of his works:

The play of this divine mind,
The union of bliss, the supreme father, and emptiness,
Is unlimited and thus beyond concept.

Cultivate a state of mind focused on bliss and emptiness as forcefully as possible. The wisdom of bliss and emptiness is compared to space, which is non-obstructive and expansive. Because they are the manifestation of the wisdom of bliss and emptiness, the substances of offering are called "offerings of Samantabhadra (All-Good)." Generally speaking, a bodhisattva named Samantabhadra is renowned for his elaborate offerings to the buddhas and bodhisattvas. But here the term All-Good (Samantabhadra) refers most appropriately to the wisdom of bliss and emptiness. It is All-Good from the viewpoint of emptiness and also from the viewpoint of bliss. This emptiness is the ultimate truth and also the ultimate virtue. And the wisdom of great bliss is the clear light wisdom: With a feeling of joy, imagine that offerings having such a nature pervade entire space.

All these objects of imagination, such as the ocean of milk in the merit field, are based on objects that we are familiar with and that we hold as valuable and good, as are the objects visualized for mandala offerings. It would be very difficult to visualize something whose appearance we do not know at all. Imagine all these various types of offerings which are the manifestation of the wisdom of bliss and emptiness. We visualize the ocean of milk because it is something within everybody's power to imagine and, I think, because humans regard it as very important and beneficial: we depend on milk right from the time of birth.

Arising through the force of your own merit and also as a manifestation of the wisdom mind of the principal deity, is a very expansive garden in the center of which is a very wide ocean of milk, with moving waves. In the center of this, visualize a wish-granting tree composed of the same seven precious stones[19] as are the balustrades of the celestial mansions. On each side visualize the two kings of the nagas, their bodies half-emerged from the ocean and in the gesture of supporting the tree.

This wish-granting tree has seven branches: one in the center and three on each side growing upwards, together forming an arbor. But if you were to look at it from outside it would look like a beautiful tree with thick branches and leaves. This wish-granting tree is beautified with leaves, flowers and fruits. In between the branches and leaves are various types of offering articles, such as the victory banners found on the golden balustrades of the celestial mansions. This tree has the capacity to fulfill wishes. In its center is a very wide, variegated lotus which has something like one hundred thousand petals, in the center of which you should visualize a very wide thorn upraised by eight lions, and on top of that a lotus with eleven layers, the lower petals broad and the upper ones narrower. The top layer has four petals. In the center of these are a lotus, and sun and moon seats, which symbolize the three principal aspects of the path.

As in the Yamantaka sadhana, although there are many different parts to the mandala, such as the cemeteries and so forth, we have to see all of them as manifestations of the wisdom mind of the central deity. All of them have special significance. We visualize the deity complete with mansion during the path, and at the time of actual arisal into an illusory body of the deity, we arise in such a form. In the same way, here you should see every part of the merit field, such as the trees and leaves, the lotuses, the throne and everything, as the manifestation of the wisdom mind of the central figure of the merit field.

The ocean of milk represents the three principles of the path; the wish-granting tree represents the qualities of the six perfections; the various flowers represent the twenty-two types of bodhicitta;[20] the fruits represent the four factors for ripening the minds of other sentient beings;[21] the two nagas represent the ultimate and conventional bodhicittas. The lions represent overpowering obstacles: the paw upholding the throne overcomes obstacles from above; the paw pressing the ground overpowers obstacles from below; and the fierce look in the eyes overcomes obstacles from the middle. All of the above have specific significance for a practitioner, so when he or she reflects upon their symbolism it has benefit. The throne should be visualized as being wide and expansive. On top of that is the lotus with eleven layers of petals.

10. ON THIS SITS MY ROOT GURU, WHO IS KIND IN
    THREE WAYS;
    IN ESSENCE ALL BUDDHAS, IN ASPECT A
    SAFFRON-ROBED MONK,
    WITH ONE FACE, TWO ARMS, RADIANT WITH
    A BRIGHT SMILE.
    HIS RIGHT HAND IS IN THE GESTURE OF EX-
    POUNDING THE DHARMA,
    HIS LEFT IN MEDITATIVE POSE HOLDS AN
    ALMS BOWL FILLED WITH NECTAR;
    HE IS DRAPED WITH THREE LUSTROUS SAF-
    FRON ROBES AND HIS HEAD IS GRACED BY
    A GOLDEN PUNDITS' HAT.

The topmost layer of this eleven-layered lotus has four petals, in the center of which sits your root guru who is kind in three ways. "Kind in three ways" indicates that the guru has given you initiation, the commentary on the tantras, and the oral instructions. This root guru should be seen as the embodiment of all the buddhas. It is said that when this text was first written by Panchen Lama Choekyi Gyaltsen, he inserted the name of his own root guru, Sangye Yeshe, here. Although one can interpret *sangye yeshe* as "the wisdom of the buddha" and not confine its connotation to the particular guru Sangye Yeshe, later the text was altered to read "in essence all the buddhas."

Visualize your guru in the aspect of a bikkshu, a fully or-dained monk, because the sangha community is a very im-portant element in buddhism. It is said that whether the Buddha's doctrine exists or not is determined by whether there is a sangha community or not. Whether or not the sutra teachings exist is determined by the presence or absence of the practice of the three bases of vinaya. The survival of tantric doctrine is determined by whether the teachings of the Guhyasamaja tantra have degenerated or not. Therefore, bikkshus are very important.

Although it is your own choice when seeking a master according to your own feeling, devotion and so on, in my opinion it is important to have a guru who is a bikkshu, especially for the followers of Lama Tsongkhapa. Actually, for the followers of the Gelug teachings there is no shortage of bikkshus at the moment. This is my personal opinion which I am expressing especially for Western dharma students.

The vows of the bikkshu have been praised not only in the vinaya treatises but also in the tantric treatises, especially those of highest yoga tantra. For example, in the Kalachakra tantra it is explained that if there are three vajra masters, a bikkshu, a novice and a layman, the bikkshu vajra master should be regarded as the highest and most important. There are even differences in the apparel distributed during the vajra master initiation. It shows how important the bikkshu is for the survival of the Buddha's doctrine. So with the realization of this great significance, here visualize the principal figure in the form of a bikkshu.

For us, the followers of Lama Tsongkhapa, although the root gurus we each visualize are by nature our respective root gurus, in appearance they should be visualized in the aspect of Lama Tsongkhapa. He is in the mudra of preaching, the posture he will adopt as the future buddha Senge Ngaro. This is auspicious for ourselves to become his disciples when he returns as the buddha to this world. He wears bikkshu robes, has one face and two arms, and is smiling. It is said that there are two causes for him to be smiling: One is that at this point we are making the most effort to engage in a virtuous practice, so he is pleased. The other is that, although our faith is very weak and we are always influenced by negativities and our actions consist mainly of negative actions, the guru is like kind parents acting as if they are pleased, even though they are not, in order to delight their naughty children. In the same way, although there is hardly any cause for him to think favorably of our actions, because we are like the children of the guru we imagine that he appears with a pleased expression.

His right hand is in the mudra of expounding the dharma. Generally speaking, the activity of preaching is an activity of the post-meditative period. His left hand is in the meditative equipoise posture. This signifies that although he is engaged in the activity of helping sentient beings, he is in meditative equipoise at the same time, an indication that he has achieved the enlightened state. In his left hand he is holding an alms bowl filled with a white nectar slightly raised in the center as Lake Manasvara is said to be. I do not know if in reality the lake is slightly higher in the middle, or if its convexity is only an illusion. So here, in the same way, visualize that the nectar is slightly higher in the middle.

Each of the guru's hands holds a flower by the stem; on the right flower is a sword and on the left a scripture. The sword, blazing with flames, represents the wisdom discriminating the nature of phenomena. The scripture on the left flower, according to some explanations, is called *The Emanated Scripture of the Ear-Whispered Transmission*. Although it might be very sacred, irrespective of whether such a scripture exists now or not, I do not think there is anything special in a scripture which is not mentioned in the eighteen volumes written by Lama Tsongkhapa himself. When Lama Tsongkhapa analyzed and set forth the meaning of tantra, especially of Guhyasamaja, he said that one has to unravel the intent of the root tantras by using the explanatory tantras, using the key of the guru's instructions. *Instructions* here refers to treatises such as Nagarjuna's *Pancha-krama* (Five Stages), *Pindikrita Sadhana*, and so forth. Lama Tsongkhapa himself said that instruction is not something which cannot be written down and which must be handed down orally. If one holds these oral kinds of instructions as too valuable and is obsessed by them, there is a danger of neglecting the great treatises which were written with great compassion and great purpose. Lama Tsongkhapa, in

the opening remarks of the *Lamrim Chenmo*, refuted the view
that there are two types of scriptures, one for scholastic studies
and one for actual practice. Such a view is mistaken. Lama
Tsongkhapa himself said that if *Lamrim Chenmo* becomes a
book for solely intellectual study, that will be the cause for
the degeneration of the doctrine. For some, hearing that there
is such an emanation scripture might be very inspiring, but
I think there may not be such a scripture apart from the eighteen volumes. But it is possible that there might be certain emanated scriptures one might be able to see when one reaches
certain levels of realization; that is a different matter. However, one should not have the attitude that because the eighteen volumes are actually printed and we can read them any-
time, we should first seek out these mysterious scriptures. Such
an attitude is greatly mistaken.

Generally I say that whether we call it the ear-whispered
doctrine or not, the main transmissions of Lama Tsongkhapa's
teachings, which are a union of sutra and tantra, are those of
the three lineages: the Sae transmission, the Ensa transmission, and the Shung transmission coming from central Tibet.
I think it is the tantric colleges who are responsible for the
perpetuation of the great transmissions of the Shungpa lineage. Since we came into exile, these colleges have been re-
established in India, and they are now among the main centers
for the study of the entire buddhist doctrine and especially
the doctrine of the union of sutra and tantra as taught by Lama
Tsongkhapa. Therefore, it is not good if the monks in the tantric colleges remain idle and unaware of this fact, or if others
do not duly honor them. If the tantric colleges are indeed the
holders of the transmissions from Lama Tsongkhapa, the manner of their doing it is as Tehor Kyorpoen Rinpoche remarked:
The monks of the tantric colleges are such that when they sit
down they practice Guhyasamaja, when they walk it is also
Guhyasamaja, and so forth. This implies that in these colleges
where the study of tantra is undertaken, such study has to be
done on the basis of Guhyasamaja, and when one actually
enters into the tantra, one has to do so on the basis of Guhya-

samaja. This is really very important. Because of the paramount importance of the Guhyasamaja practice, Lama Tsongkhapa wrote five volumes on it. He must have composed them with the purpose of benefiting sentient beings so that they could actualize the resultant state of omniscience. The Guhyasamaja volumes are not meant only for developing understanding of the doctrine or tantra in general; therefore, they must have a special significance and purpose.

I often say that it is wrong that someone who claims himself to be a Gelugpa is content only with the recitation of *Lama Choepa* and Vajrayogini, and neglects practices like Guhyasamaja and so forth; that is not good. Some persons, having studied Yamantaka, Guhyasamaja and Heruka for many years, when it comes to the actual practice neglect all their study and become pre-occupied with a very short text and ritual. That is actually a disgrace. It is a different case if your root guru sees that you have a special affinity with a particular deity and has advised you to emphasize that practice. But if you neglect these main practices through laziness and misunderstanding, it is a grave mistake.

A friend of mine once told me, "I asked some Gelugpa monks about Guhyasamaja; they said, 'We don't know much about Guhyasamaja.' When I pressed them further, 'Is Guhyasamaja not a main practice of Gelug?', they replied, 'No, it is only Yamantaka and Vajrayogini which are important.' " That shows that the practice of Guhyasamaja is degenerating. I think Yamantaka and Guhyasamaja and Chakrasamvara are very important. As for Chakrasamvara, the tradition of Luipa is very important; Lama Tsongkhapa regards it as the root of Heruka tantra. And Ghantapa's tradition has a very unique feature in that it contains the process of initiation into the body mandala. Lama Tsongkhapa himself composed the manual of initiation into the Ghantapa body mandala; therefore it has a special significance.

These are some side remarks I am making in relation to the question of the said *Emanated Scripture of the Ear-Whispered Transmission*. So, if we think more about this mysterious scripture, it will just dissolve into light! Anyway, if you are studying or meditating on lamrim, visualize that scripture as *Lamrim Chenmo*; and if you are putting more emphasis on the study of tantra, then imagine it is the *Ngagrim Chenmo* (Great Exposition on Tantra). If you are studying *Prajnaparamita*, it could be visualized as *The Eight Thousand Verse Perfection of Wisdom Sutra*; if you are studying madhyamaka, visualize it as a madhyamaka scripture; if you are emphasizing pramana, visualize it as a scripture of pramana, and so forth, appropriate to your own study and practice.

I wonder whether the flowers being held by Lama Tsongkhapa are lotuses or not. In Guhyasamaja, the male deities hold lotuses and the females utpalas. I have checked and I think they are utpalas. When I was a child, someone brought me a flower called *utpala*—it looked very distinctive. There is a flower called a Himalayan poppy in English which is said to also be a type of utpala, but it is quite different. If we assume that the ones visualized here are not the type growing in Himalayan regions, then we could take it that they are a very special type of utpala. The point is to visualize the most beautiful and perfect flowers. The guru is adorned with the three types of saffron-colored robes and is wearing a hat which is the color of gold. The tip is very pointed, representing the correct view of emptiness.

11. IN HIS HEART SITS THE ALL-PERVADING LORD VAJRADHARA, WITH A BLUE-COLORED BODY,
    ONE FACE AND TWO ARMS, HOLDING VAJRA AND BELL AND EMBRACING VAJRADHATU ISHVARI;
    THEY DELIGHT IN THE PLAY OF SIMULTANEOUS VOIDNESS AND BLISS,
    ARE ADORNED WITH JEWELLED ORNAMENTS OF MANY DESIGNS AND ARE CLOTHED IN GARMENTS OF HEAVENLY SILKS.

At the heart of Guru Lozang, who is your own guru in the aspect of Lama Tsongkhapa, visualize Guru Shakyamuni, who is the master of the doctrine. He should be visualized as thumb-sized or four finger-widths high. The small size helps to overcome mental sinking and scattering, thus allowing you to have stronger concentration. If that is not within your ability, he should be visualized slightly larger. Lord Buddha is showing his normal hand gestures, left hand in meditative posture and right hand touching the ground. At his heart, visualize Vajradhara, the master of tantra, with consort, about one finger-width high. At his heart visualize the concentration being, the syllable HUM, which is the source of all phenomena included within samsara and nirvana. It is by nature the very subtle wind and mind and is radiating light rays of five colors. The HUM, being blue, represents immutability and Akshobhya. Although it is of blue color it radiates five different colors: from the nada blue, from the drop white, from the crescent yellow, from the HA red, from the U green. As found in a commentary on the generation stage, visualize Vajradhara as being heavy, and the concentration being, the syllable HUM, as very small and just like the filament in a light bulb—very, very thin, bluish, but very bright. This will help you to have clarity of mind and prevent mental sinking. If you visualize Vajradhara as though he were heavy, it will help you prevent mental distraction.

The consort Vajra Ishvari is also holding a bell and vajra while embracing Vajradhara. Both are adorned with precious jewel ornaments, and are absorbed in the ecstasy of great bliss. The bodies of Vajradhara and the consort are adorned with the major and minor noble marks, and light rays are radiating from them. Imagine that, at the tips of all these light rays, many different emanations are being created, emitting out and returning and so forth. The deity is constantly engaged in the activity of creating these emanations to help sentient beings. Also, Vajradhara could be visualized in reality being the particular meditational deity in which you specialize. He is seen as seated in the vajrasana position; the significance of this is related to the realization of what is known as the four types of vajrasana positions[22] that has preceded his achievement of buddhahood.

Such a being is called *Lama* because in reality he is your guru, *Lozang* because he has the appearance of Lama Tsongkhapa (Lozang Tragpa), *Thubwang* because he has Buddha Shakyamuni at his heart, and *Dorje Chang* because at Buddha's heart is Vajradhara. Therefore he is called Lama Lozang Thubwang Dorje Chang.

12. RADIANT WITH THOUSANDS OF LIGHT RAYS, ADORNED WITH THE MAJOR AND MINOR SIGNS,
THE GURU SITS IN THE VAJRA POSITION ENHALOED BY A FIVE-COLORED RAINBOW.
HIS PURIFIED AGGREGATES ARE THE FIVE BUDDHAS GONE-TO-BLISS;
HIS FOUR ELEMENTS, THE FOUR CONSORTS;
HIS SENSE SPHERES, ENERGY CHANNELS.
SINEWS AND JOINTS ARE IN ACTUALITY BODHISATTVAS;
THE HAIRS OF HIS PORES ARE TWENTY-ONE THOUSAND ARHATS;
HIS LIMBS ARE WRATHFUL PROTECTORS;
THE LIGHT RAYS ARE DIRECTIONAL GUARDIANS, LORDS OF WEALTH AND THEIR ATTENDANTS;
WHILE WORLDLY GODS ARE BUT CUSHIONS FOR HIS FEET.

This is the visualization of the body mandala deities. It explains how the elements and sources and so forth should be generated into deities. I have found that one of the commentaries says that if one's root guru is alive, the visualization of the mandala deities at his bodily parts as explained here actually constitutes a complete body mandala practice. In Guhyasamaja, in the section related to entering into union with a consort, it is said that if the consort is an action seal, a live consort, visualizing deities on her body becomes an actual body mandala practice. But if one is entering into union with a visualized consort, it does not. So, in the same way, when one's spiritual guru is alive, due to the force of his actually having these elements and so on, such visualization may be a body mandala practice; whereas when he is no longer alive, as far as one's ordinary perception is concerned, he has dissolved these physical elements and so forth which are the basis of the body mandala. But I cannot state that this is definitely so.

The placement of the deities of the body mandala explained in the *Kachem Lung Kurma* commentary is quite different from that mentioned in the transmission of the commentary on Guhyasamaja from Amdo, but I do not think there is any contradiction. At the crown is Vairochana, at the throat Amitabha, at the heart Akshobhya, at the navel Ratnasambhava, and at the groin Amoghasiddhi. According to the commentary on Guhyasamaja, one should visualize them in a straight line, just like a pole, the crown of each deity touching the seat of the deity above it. But according to the *Kachem Lung Kurma* commentary it is somewhat different: the deities are slightly smaller so that they are not touching each other.

The four elements are transformed into the four consorts: at the navel in front of Ratnasambhava is Lochana; in front of Akshobhya at the heart, Mamaki; in front of Amitabha, between the two channel wheels of the throat and the heart, at the point where the wheel of fire is said to be, Pandaravasin; in front of Vairochana, Tara.

There are two traditions regarding the dhyani buddhas: in one, they are embracing the consorts, in the other they are not embracing, but only facing them.

Now to describe the sources (the eye source, nose source and so forth). In the center of the two eye organs are Kshitigarbhas facing outwards, embraced by Rupavajras. On the two ears are Vajrapanis embraced by Shabdavajras; at the nose is Akashagarbha embraced by Gandhavajra; at the tongue, Lokeshvara embraces Rasavajra; and at the heart, behind Akshobhya, is Manjushri without a consort. In the *Kachem Lung Kurma* commentary, it says that Manjushri is in union with Vajra Ishvari, in which case there would be thirty-three deities. Although Varja Ishvari is mentioned in the root tantra, here we are following the practice of Guhyasamaja Akshobhyavajra based upon the explanation found in the *Vajramala*, in which there is no mention of Vajra Ishvari. But the *Kachem Lung Kurma* commentary explains that one should visualize Vajra Ishvari as the consort of Manjushri, white in color, having three faces—white, blue and red—and six arms, the first two arms embracing Manjushri, the remaining right arms holding a reality source[23] and a sword, and the left carrying a lotus and jewel. At the secret organ is Sarvanivarana-viskambhini embraced by Sparshavajra. At the eight major joints are Samantabhadras, just as explained during the initiation. One way to visualize them is to place them on the joints of the shoulders, elbows, and wrists—three on each of the arms, making six—and on the ankles, knees, and hips—six on the legs—together making twelve. Another version is to visualize one Samantabhadra at the sternum and then visualize his reflections at all the three hundred and sixty joints. You can imagine that these deities are there. Although the five goddesses are not mentioned here explicitly, they should be visualized as found in the Guhyasamaja commentary, embracing the bodhisattvas as described.

At the crown is Maitreya, the purified aspect of the channels. According to the commentary on Guhyasamaja that we are following, he is visualized behind Vairochana. So, the rearmost is Maitreya, in front of him Vairochana, then Tara embracing him, and in front Ushnishachakravartin. So, there are four deities at the crown. But according to *Kachem Lung Kurma*, these four deities are visualized one above the other with Vairochana below, then Maitreya, and on top Ushnishachakravartin. Doesn't the system of Guhyasamaja seem more convenient? Otherwise we would have to shift from one system when practicing Guhyasamaja to the other for *Lama Choepa*, which would be quite confusing. According to Pelmang Koenchog Gyaltsen's writings, which are based on a commentary on *Lama Choepa* he received from Koenchog Jigme Wangpo, the placement of the body mandala deities is done according to the commentary on Guhyasamaja. So, for those of us who are quite familiar with the practice of Guhyasamaja it is better to do it as found there. But you can follow either of these two traditions—as found in the commentary on Guhyasamaja, or as found here in this commentary on *Lama Choepa*.

Here it says that the *bhapu* (hairs of the pores) of the body should be visualized as arhats, but because their number does not tally with the number of pores of the body, it is said that *bhapu* should be taken to mean the hairs. I wonder why the hairs are not mentioned explicitly? I do not know whether in Tsangpa dialect the word for hairs is the same as that for pores.

The text goes on to talk of the limbs arising into the ten wrathful deities, the purified aspects of the ten consciousnesses. These consciousnesses are not the ones referred to in the abhidharma texts, but are, rather, different instances of the one mind of bliss and emptiness. On the right hand is Yamantakrit, on the left Aparajita. Your visualization of them should not be so fixed or rigid so that when you move your hands these deities fall off! It is said that if one is concerned about them falling, then when one moves one's hands one should imagine that the deities move with them. But you should not worry too much about them falling! For example, in the visualization of the protection circle, Sumbharaja is in an upside-down position as he guards the practitioner from harmful underground spirits.

In the commentary *Kachem Lung Kurma* it says that Hayagriva is at the root of the tongue, but it is better, as in the Guhyasamaja commentary, to visualize him outside the mouth, because wrathful deities are forces to counter the interferences, so should be emerging, not hiding inside! It would seem unnecessary to visualize the wrathful deities if all they do is hide. According to this commentary, the wrathful one at the vajra organ is visualized inside, but it is better to visualize it outside as well.

The light rays are visualized as the fifteen directional guardians. Light rays radiate from the heart of the central figure into the ten directions, just as in the Yamantaka and Guhyasamaja sadhanas. At the tips of these light rays are the directional guardians, who are by nature the wisdom of the central figure. It is said that one should visualize yakshas as their retinues but this could be omitted.

One interpretation of the worldly deities being like a seat is that the worldly deities are pleased to be even at the feet of the central figure. But according to Pelmang Koenchog Gyaltsen's explanation, you should visualize worldly deities such as Brahma, Indra and so forth below, but on the seat, just as in Yamantaka, where various worldly deities are below his feet. You should not have the notion that they are being suppressed, being trodden on and inflicted with sufferings, but rather that they are being taken care of by the principal deity and are guarded from indulging in non-virtuous actions. Artists sometimes must take many things into consideration when painting thankas, and so some artists may draw these worldly deities seated on the lotus below the deity; this is wrong. They should be under the feet of the central figure, on the seat. If you take the viewpoint that these worldly deities have been taken into the care of the central figure, that will also help you to be invulnerable to their harms, for even if they should wish to harm you they will not dare.

13. SURROUNDING HIM IN THEIR RESPECTIVE ORDER SIT THE DIRECT AND LINEAGE GURUS,
YIDAMS, HOSTS OF MANDALA DEITIES,
BUDDHAS, BODHISATTVAS, HEROES AND DAKINIS,
ENCIRCLED BY AN OCEAN OF DHARMA PROTECTORS.

Having visualized the central figure, around him visualize the root and lineage gurus as described here. A light ray radiates from the heart of the central figure, narrow at the start and becoming very broad. At the tip, visualize your own root guru surrounded by the gurus from whom you have received teachings directly. If possible, you should include all your teachers, including the teacher who first taught you how to read the alphabet. If you can manage it, it is good to view all of them as your own guru and also see them as buddhas. I normally advise Westerners that if one takes initiation from someone, there is no choice but to regard that person as a teacher. But in other cases, if one has not had the opportunity to examine the teacher and cannot do so without taking commentaries (excluding tantric teachings) or general teachings such as introductions to buddhism from that teacher, as an exception these can be listened to in the same way as lectures. Then, when one thinks one can accept him as a teacher, rely on him and observe the commitments, one should do so. So, it is important to understand how to go about relating to spiritual teachers according to the situation.

The root guru faces you; but according to some versions, one can visualize the root guru facing the central figure. During an initiation, although there is just one central deity, that deity assumes an aspect called the "action vajra," an attendant who performs activities. In the same way here, although your root guru is visualized as the central figure of the merit field, you can also visualize him in his usual appearance. His particular function is to help recommend you for acceptance by the central figure. You can visualize body mandala deities on the body of the root guru, according to the deity yoga in which you specialize.

Visualize another two light rays, one radiating towards the left and one to the right. On the central figure's right, visualize Maitreya surrounded by the lineage gurus of the vast practice in one group. On the left is Manjushri surrounded by the lineage gurus of the profound practice. Below each of these groups is the lineage of the Kadam masters. From Atisha the lineages of the vast and profound practices merged into one; therefore the Kadam lineage is visualized on both sides. Due to different ways of expounding the doctrine, this Kadam lineage is divided into three lineages: Kadam Shungpawa, Lamrimpa and Mengagpa, stemming from Potowa, Gompowa and Chekawa respectively. Therefore, there are these three groups of lineage gurus on both sides. These three lineages eventually merged into one from Lama Tsongkhapa; therefore there is a further group of lineage gurus. There is a complete set on either side, one below Maitreya and one below Manjushri. It is said that one should also visualize an empty throne which signifies the continual advent of masters of the doctrine.

If you are emphasizing the practice of lojong on the basis of the *Bodhisattvacharyavatara*, visualize the lineage gurus of what is called the lineage of extensive actions; then it is not necessary to visualize Maitreya, but rather you should visualize Manjushri, Nagarjuna, Shantideva and so forth.

What is meant by "the lineage gurus of the experiential inspiration"? According to Pelmang Koenchog Gyaltsen, there are various interpretations. He says that, according to Karto, this phrase refers to the lineage gurus of the particular meditational deity that one emphasizes in one's practice, whereas Purchog Jhampa Rinpoche identifies it with the lineage gurus of the Kadam's sixteen drop practice. Hence, for a practitioner who has no initiation into the Kadam sixteen drops, there is no need to visualize the gurus of this lineage.

Purchog Jhampa Rinpoche is the one who said, "Because I am from eastern Tibet and have a very tall body, when I prostrate I have the great advantage of covering more ground, and so I create more merits." (It is said that the more ground one covers with one's body when prostrating, the greater the merit.) Purchog Jhampa Rinpoche performed prostrations on a daily basis even when he was very old. Gungtang Rinpoche wrote in his biography that he used to prostrate something like a thousand times daily. It is really amazing to hear of these feats, and the extent of the hardships these men underwent in performing their practices. These masters did not undertake such extensive prostrations merely for the sake of physical exercise!

The tradition which was explained by Kyabje Trijang Rinpoche is very good. Because there are many different explanations regarding the lineage gurus, the former Dalai Lama asked Kyabje Pabongka Rinpoche for clarification on this topic. Although in paintings the five groups of tantric lineage gurus are arranged in five straight lines, one next to the other, I think when you visualize them they should be placed above the four petals of the top-most layer of the lotus as follows. On the front petal, visualize either Guhyasamaja, the king of tantras, or Yamantaka. Although Yamantaka belongs to the father tantra, because it has the essential features of both father and mother tantras complete, and because Yamantaka is also a very special deity of the Gelug tradition, he can be visualized on the front petal. On the right is Guhyasamaja, the king of father tantra, or Yamantaka, if Guhyasamaja has been placed on the front petal. On the left is Heruka, the king of mother tantra. On the rear petal are the mandala deities of the sixteen drops of Kadam. If you have not received the initiation of the Kadam sixteen drops, visualize Hevajra. Or, if you are mainly meditating on Kalachakra, you can visualize Kalachakra there. You can change around the meditational deities according to your emphasis on particular deities. Thus, there are five groups of tantric lineage gurus. In the center visualize the gurus of the mahamudra lineage. Whether one calls it a Gelug and Kagyud lineage or a Gelug lineage, this guru yoga practice, *Lama Choepa*, is like an uncommon preliminary practice to mahamudra meditation. Although the gurus of the mahamudra lineage are by nature individual, all of them are visualized in the aspect of Manjushri.

To summarize: The mahamudra lineage gurus are above the central figure of the merit field; those of Yamantaka above Yamantaka in front; Guhyasamaja on the right; Heruka on the left; and the lineage gurus of the sixteen drops of Kadam, or of Hevajra, as appropriate, above the rear petal.

Within the sixteen drops of Kadam mandala there are various deities belonging to different classes of tantra, including deities of highest yoga tantra, such as Guhyasamaja of the

Jnanapata school. In this mandala, there are some Tibetan masters such as Kutoen Tsoendru Yongdrung and Ngok Legpai Sherab. Khedup Rinpoche, in his text called *Thubten Jithor* (Dusting the Buddha's Doctrine), said that Tibetan gurus should not be visualized inside a mandala; therefore, he had some reservations about this practice. There was at one time even a controversy about whether the father scriptures and son scriptures of Kadam are authentic teachings or not. In the biography of the First Dalai Lama, we find that after someone said to him, "I have heard that the father and the son scriptures of Kadam are not authentic," he replied, "I don't know whether they are authentic or not, but they actually are helpful for the mind." This is really a very direct reply, because if something is helpful for training the mind it proves it is an authentic dharma teaching; what further qualities are needed?

So, on the four petals of the first layer are four meditational deities of highest yoga tantra. Although in paintings only the deities are drawn, if possible you should visualize the entire celestial mansion as well. But if that is beyond your capability, it is a different matter. If you do visualize the celestial mansions, then at the point where the four initiations are taken you can perform the self-initiation of the deity in conjunction with this guru yoga. For example, on the front petal, visualize the entire mandala of Yamantaka, whether it be the solitary hero or the thirteen deity; on the right Guhyasamaja; on the left Heruka, in the form in which you specialize. If it is the tradition of Luipa, visualize the Luipa mandala, or if the body mandala according to the Ghantapa tradition, visualize that. If it is easier, visualize them facing towards you, but if it is not disturbing and is just as convenient, it is better to visualize them facing towards the central figure, just as the retinue all face the central deity of the mandala.

I think one can visualize either the celestial mansions of the meditational deities within the merit field on the tree of assembly, or the entire tree enclosed within a celestial mansion.

On the second layer of the lotus petal, visualize Kalachakra in front and on the rest of the petals the various deities of

highest yoga tantra, such as the red Yamantaka, the Guhyasamaja according to Jnanapata, and the various aspects of
Heruka. There are many different aspects of Heruka and so
on, and many different tantras of which I do not even know
the names! It is very amazing to read a text such as the Sakya
text *The Compendium of the Tantras* in which are mentioned
innumerable deities. As this practice is regarded as a Gelug
guru yoga, most of the deities which are well known in the
Gelug system are visualized. But if your practice is integrated
with practices of other sects, you can visualize the deities found
in those other sects, such as Hayagriva and so on. You should
not have the rigid notion that the deities belonging to certain
sects cannot be included in the merit field of any particular
practice. On their part, the objects of refuge could not have
any sectarian attitudes! The point is that those in whom one
has great faith and interest are visualized and placed on the
merit field.

Below, on the third layer, visualize the deities of yoga tantra, Vajradhatu (Dorje Ying) being the main one. The practice of this deity has degenerated in the Gelug system, and
I think it is important to restore it because an understanding
of yoga tantra as explained in Tsongkhapa's *Ngagrim Chenmo*
is impossible without a good knowledge of Vajradhatu. The
understanding of Kunrig[24] alone does not get one far. Below
this layer are the deities of performance (charya) tantra, and
then come the deities of action (kriya) tantra. In the mandala
of Vairochana Sambodhi, there are certain arhats, so I do not
see why one can visualize Indian masters and not Tibetan
masters inside the mandala! But Khedup Rinpoche must have
had some reason to say that one should not. Within action
tantra there are many different deities belonging to the various lineages: the lotus, vajra, jewel and tathagata.

Below are the thousand buddhas of the fortunate eon and
so forth in this order. Although the deities visualized above
are also considered buddhas, they are placed in this order
because—of the two vehicles—the tantric vehicle is regarded
as higher. The ordering does not mean that meditational dei-

ties are higher than buddhas.

Below the buddhas, visualize the bodhisattvas such as the eight bodhisattva disciples of Buddha Shakyamuni. Below these are arhats such as the sixteen arhats, and then the heroes and heroines. One tradition places heroes on the right side and heroines on the left; in another heroes and heroines are arranged alternately; and a third system has them embracing each other. Below the heroes and heroines come the dharmapalas. The main Gelug dharmapalas are the three dharmapalas of the three scopes. In his *Geden Tenpa Gyepai Monlam*, Gungtang Rinpoche said:

> The main protectors of the three scopes are
> Mahakala, Vaisravana and Kalarupa—
> Through your power, Mighty Dharmapalas,
> May the tradition of Victorious Lozang always flourish!

Mahakala is a wrathful aspect of Avalokiteshvara and therefore is the dharmapala who is especially pleased by those who observe pure morality, and as the practice of morality is the chief practice of those of middling scope he is regarded as their dharmapala. Because, in the practice of the lower scope, following the law of cause and effect is emphasized, Kalarupa is regarded as the dharmapala of the lowest scope. In the Gelug tradition one seeks the protection of the dharmapala corresponding to one's own practice. I think that Mahakala and Kalarupa are the main dharma protectors of the Gelug lineage, as attested by the practices undertaken in the two tantric colleges. In Gyudmed College mainly Kalarupa is practiced and in the Upper Tantric College it is Mahakala. I think the tantric colleges make a great contribution to the dharma, because it is due to them that we have the continuity of the transmission of the teachings of Guhyasamaja. Between Mahakala and Kalarupa, I think the uncommon dharmapala is Kalarupa. There is a saying that for the Gelug tradition the guru is Manjushri, the meditational deity is Manjushri and the dharmapala is also Manjushri. Of the external, internal and secret aspects of Kalarupa, the internal aspect is regarded as the chief one. Lama Tsongkhapa composed the famous praise hymns "Kyang Kuma" to the internal aspect of Kalarupa.

Actually there is no need for any dharmapala besides these three. Sometimes I say that only when we hear that Kalarupa has passed away will we have to seek some other protection. Although Lama Lozang Thubwang Dorje Chang does not have any partiality or prejudice, if you make fervent prayers while viewing him as the embodiment of the meditational deity, the Buddha, the dharmapala and everything, the inspiration you receive will be more powerful. In the same way, if you relate to a dharmapala like Kalarupa and entrust yourself completely to his protection, then there will be a special power in that relationship. It is not very good to neglect the dharmapalas that were specifically practiced by Lama Tsongkhapa himself and assigned to protect his doctrine. Neglecting them and going to other dharmapalas is, I think, quite mistaken and should not be the general mode of procedure of Gelug practitioners. There might be unusual cases where high beings have their own individual dharmapalas due to their realizations, but such cases should be taken as exceptions. I have made many observations on this topic, all through my own personal experiences. Therefore, these three dharmapalas of the three scopes should be regarded as the most important.

There are many other dharmapala mentioned in the tantras, such as the four-armed Mahakala and Chamseng. Generally speaking, although a means of inferring someone's realizations through what is called the "signs of irreversibility" is explained in scriptures[25], such realization is very difficult to judge. So then, how difficult it would be to judge a dharmapala! Paelden Lhamo was not a special protector of the Gelug tradition, and Lama Tsongkhapa did not have any special relationship with her, but the First Dalai Lama, Gedun Drub, did, and appointed her as a chief dharmapala at Tashi Lhunpo monastery. Gedun Gyatso, being the reincarnation of Gedun Drub, related mainly to Paelden Lhamo. He served as an abbot of both Sera and Drepung monasteries and, because of that, Paelden Lhamo also became one of the chief dharmapalas in Drepung. Because many Gelug monasteries were established in the eastern part of Tibet and in Amdo and so on as branches of Sera and Drepung, the practice of Paelden Lhamo became very widespread in monasteries such as Amdo Tashi Khyil and Kumbum. The practice of dharmapala Nechung also became widespread in the branch monasteries of Drepung.

The supermundane dharmapalas with whom you have the main relationship should be visualized on the merit field. There is no special reason why you should place each and every dharmapala there. The Seventh Dalai Lama and Phurchog Nagawang Jhampa said very emphatically that if one places worldly dharmapalas on the merit field there is a danger of annulling one's practice of refuge. For example, although I have a very special relationship with Gyalpo Kunga, I would not place him in the merit field; if I did, it would be a degeneration of my refuge practice. Although these types of dharmapalas are regarded as being in reality or in ultimate aspect manifestations of the five dhyani buddhas, they have arisen into specific worldly forms for a specific purpose. Therefore we should relate to them on that level also and should not entrust ourselves entirely to them, especially for our ultimate aims. This is applicable to other worldly protectors too: we can seek protection and assistance from them, but not entrust ourselves entirely to their care and guidance.

It seems that the way in which the practitioner should relate to these dharmapalas has been explained in the tantras. If you can actually maintain a very strong divine pride of the meditational deity as the yogis themselves do, then you can relate to these dharmapalas in the proper manner and employ them for many essential activities. But for persons like ourselves, I find the Kadam approach very good. The Kadampas' practice of dharma encompasses the three scopes, or the three trainings, and they have only four deities: (1) Buddha Shakyamuni, the master of the doctrine; (2) Avalokiteshvara, the deity of compassion; (3) Tara, the deity of activities; and (4) Miyowa, the deity for eliminating obstacles. It is really practical. For them, the definitive or the ultimate dharmapala is the law of cause and effect, because it is the law of cause and effect which determines our fate and which can protect us from harms and so forth. Therefore, observe the law of karma well and, if you can, strive to develop realizations within your mental continuum instead of getting caught up in the complex practices of too many dharmapalas. It is actually a lot better. If one has the necessary realization for relating to dharmapalas as explained in the tantras, then it is a different matter and one can relate to all kinds of dharmapalas, whether they belong to the supermundane or the mundane levels. Such a yogi would be able to employ them positively for helping other sentient beings. The biography of the Second Dalai Lama, Gedun Gyatso, testifies to his special emphasis on the practice of the dharmapalas. He considered it as one of his main practices, saying that in general while performing these rituals one should focus upon the welfare of all the sentient beings of the three realms. Although he could not claim that he was doing this, he nevertheless did keep in his heart the well-being of all the living beings on this planet. So, for those who have high realizations, it is a different matter. For us who do not have the realizations for relating to dharmapalas as outlined in the tantras, thus lacking the power to command them as we desire, requests to the dharmapalas have to be done more as a kind of supplication. In that respect, it is better to make the request to the law of cause and effect.

In the Gelug system much emphasis is placed on what is called *the validity of conventional appearance*; it is very important, as it is the basis upon which one follows the law of cause and effect. It is generally said that the view of the Great Perfection School, dzogchen, is explained from the viewpoint of the resultant state, and the Sakyas' view, called *the union of clarity and emptiness*, is explained from the viewpoint of the path, and Lama Tsongkhapa's view of emptiness is from the viewpoint of taking the ordinary, usual appearance of phenomena into account. Because it is left to one's own discretion whether or not one wants to practice dharma, everyone has the freedom to choose one's own meditational deity, and likewise whether one relates to a particular dharmapala or not is also left to one's own discretion. But in regard to the question of the general welfare of Tibet and the Tibetan government and so on, I think it is more important to practice Paelden Lhamo and Gyalpo Kunga than other dharmapalas. I think for a Gelugpa, dharmapala Kalarupa is the most important.

These remarks do not imply that these worldly dharmapalas and the local spirits and so forth should not be propitiated, but rather suggest that one's attitude towards them should be that of seeking assistance, just as one seeks the assistance of friends and so forth—one does not entrust oneself completely and seek refuge in them. So, if you have a personal relationship with such dharmapalas you should relate to them in that way and you will receive the benefits of their activities in return. Kyabje Trijang Rinpoche once told me of a medium in Tibet who was in a trance wearing one of those spirit hats; Kyabje Rinpoche asked him, "Who are you?", and he replied, "I'm Geshe Potowa"!

In Tibet there is a tradition of burning incense called *sangsol* (burning of huge incense); if we look at it purely from the viewpoint of buddhist principles, there is not much significance to it. But I think certain substances have specific power in themselves, so there is actually some benefit in doing it. For example, if there is a bad smell pervading a room and we burn incense, the smell is cleared. Especially in Tibet where there has·been desecration on a massive scale, this practice of burning incense helps; and it also demonstrates externally the Tibetans' determination to continue the practice of dharma!

The subject of the fifteen directional guardians is very complex because there are two aspects, one belonging to the worldly and another belonging to the supermundane level. Sometimes I feel that we can conjure up a lot of things merely through our ideas. I find this very complex. Regarding the four directional guardians, although they are worldly protectors, they were entrusted with the responsibility of protecting the dharma as assistants to the sixteen arhats. They took this oath from

the Buddha himself, but they are nevertheless worldly dharmapalas so cannot be placed in the merit field, and therefore
are visualized amidst clouds in the four directions.

14. THE THREE DOORS OF EACH ARE MARKED
    WITH THE THREE VAJRAS;
    FROM THEIR *HUM* SYLLABLES HOOKED LIGHT
    RAYS RADIATE AND
    DRAW FORTH THE WISDOM BEINGS FROM
    THEIR NATURAL ABODES
    AND THEY BECOME INSEPARABLY SET.

If you can, you should visualize the three syllables, which are
symbols for the three vajras—vajra body, speech and mind—
at the three parts of the bodies of each of the figures of the
merit field. If that is unmanageable, you should visualize these
three syllables at the three parts of the body of the central figure, Lama Lozang Thubwang Dorje Chang. As explained during the initiation, the indivisibility of the vajra body, vajra
speech and vajra mind is very important. Light rays in the
shapes of hooks emanate from the syllable HUM. There are
three meanings of "natural abodes." The first refers to the
expanse of reality, the sphere of the truth body, from where
the wisdom beings are requested to come and take a form body.
The second is that these beings arise into an emanation body
from the natural abode of the enjoyment body, and the third
refers to their resident abode. The visualization of inviting wisdom beings is to help one's own attitude. It is not the case
that these commitment beings are lifeless dolls and the subsequent dissolution of the wisdom beings makes them come alive.
As the commitment beings were already visualized as having
arisen from the wisdom of bliss and emptiness when they were
generated, technically speaking there is no need to make them
more special by dissolving the wisdom beings into them. But,
because we are accustomed to our habitual preconceptions,
this method of inviting wisdom beings and dissolving them
into the commitment beings was devised. Otherwise it does

not make much sense. If one does not have faith, inviting wisdom beings will not help.

15. O SOURCES OF GOODNESS AND WELL-BEING
    THROUGHOUT THE THREE TIMES,
    O, ROOT AND LINEAGE GURUS, YIDAMS, THREE
    JEWELS OF REFUGE,
    HEROES, DAKINIS, DHARMA PROTECTORS AND
    HOSTS OF GUARDIANS;
    BY THE POWER OF YOUR COMPASSION COME
    FORTH AND ABIDE STEADFASTLY!

This is the verse of invitation. I think it was composed by Khedup Sangye Yeshe. In the text that we usually employ as a manual, it explains that the gurus of the three times are the source of all accomplishments and so forth. We request them to appear in front of us through the force of their compassion to be our field of accumulating merit.

16. THOUGH ALL THINGS ARE TOTALLY FREE OF
    INHERENT COMING AND GOING,
    STILL YOU ARISE THROUGH THE ACTION OF
    WISDOM AND LOVING-COMPASSION,
    ACCORDING TO THE DISPOSITIONS OF THE
    VARIED DISCIPLES;
    O, HOLY SAVIORS, PLEASE COME FORTH WITH
    YOUR ENTOURAGES.

This verse explains that the nature of all phenomena is emptiness and that there is no phenomenon which has inherent existence, and that the same is true of the subjective omniscient mind which, because it pervades all phenomena, is free of going from one to another. Nevertheless, since sentient beings are of different dispositions and have different interests, the truth body appears appropriately in many different manifestations. So, we request the truth body to arise in these multitudinous forms as the field of our merit.

17. OM GURU BUDDHA BODHISATTVA DHAR-
MAPALA SAPARIWARA E HYE HIH
DZA HUH BAM HOH!
THE WISDOM BEINGS AND SYMBOLIC BEINGS
BECOME NON-DUAL.

Dza hum bam hoh draws forth the wisdom beings and then dissolves them into the commitment beings. Doing this involves four stages: invoking, or drawing forth, the wisdom beings; their absorption into the commitment beings; binding, which means merging, or dissolving; and being pleased, which means becoming joyously inseparable. That is the meaning of these four syllables. You should visualize that a complete set of the merit field as wisdom beings is dissolved into each and every individual figure of the merit field. This will help you see each figure of the merit field as the embodiment of the entire merit field. All of them, although having different appearances, are actually manifestations of the one wisdom mind of the central figure.

I think there is a special import in the fact that the one mind, the wisdom mind, of the central figure appears as the companions (sangha), as the meditational deities who grant the supreme feats, as the gurus who grant inspiration, as heroes and heroines who provide assistance on the path, as dharmapalas to protect one from obstacles, and as the buddhas, bodhisattvas and arhats—or sravakas—in order to tame individuals such as ourselves. Although from the point of view of tantra there is no special reason why these arhats should be included, they are visualized here on the basis of the general buddhist path. Here, although they are in the appearance of sravakas, by nature they, too, are the manifestation of the central figure. I think this arrangement of the merit field and the various figures within it has been made on the basis of the entirety of sutra and tantra practices, so it includes all the objects of refuge connected with both vehicles. The guru Vajradhara has taken all these various appearances in order to tame ordinary beings like us, all the way from enabling us to obtain the proper form of existence for practicing the path, through to helping us to reach the final achievement of enlightenment.

In one of the writings of the Fifth Dalai Lama, there is actually some criticism of having these hosts of different figures in *Lama Choepa*. But I think there is a special significance in visualizing all these merit field figures. However, on the other hand there is also a special significance to simple merit field visualizations such as found in *Six Session Guru Yoga*. In order to tame our very coarse states of mind, Guru Vajradhara has taken all these different forms to apply all types of skillful means. I think if you can take this viewpoint, it will help a lot in realizing the great kindness of the guru. For example, if you have a friend who for your sake has approached people at different levels, going to the higher ones and being polite and meeting the lower ones and being more direct, you would regard that friend as very kind, and would feel very indebted to him. But if on the other hand you have a friend who is not very skillful, although he has pure motivation there is a danger he might let you down. Therefore, Guru Vajradhara has taken these different forms such as meditational deities, heroes and heroines, dakinis, buddhas and bodhisattvas and the deities of the lower tantras and so forth. If you understand this fact, you will see a special significance in the "one-pointed prayer"[26] to the gurus that follows later, in which one says that the guru is one's dakini and dharmapala. All this shows the inexhaustible skillful means of the guru for taming just one sentient being. You should not have the notion that many different beings have gathered here to tame one person such as yourself, but rather you should understand that because your ignorance and preconceptions are infinite, in order to tame you the one guru-deity has issued all these different forms. So, cultivate great faith.

4 Seven-Limbed Practice

As far as the members of the merit field are concerned, there is none higher than or superior to the guru. And for the actual process of accumulating merit, there is no better practice than the seven-limbed practice. The purpose of accumulating merit is to achieve the highest enlightenment. The meaning of enlightenment is not that one passes away. It is rather ironic that in Tibetan someone who is stupid or naive is jokingly called the "completely enlightened one"! I think this shows too much familiarity with the dharma! Similarly, *Lama Koenchog* (Lama Jewel) is actually a nickname for a really stupid person, even though there is no better name! We accumulate merit for the purpose of achieving enlightenment, and what is meant by the enlightened state is a state free of all obstructions to omniscience and liberation. A being of such a state would be able to perceive the entire expanse of phenomena in just a single moment of consciousness, for he is free of all the obscurations to knowledge. As Chandrakirti, in his autocommentary on *Madhyamakavatara*, says: "Without ever touching the object itself you realize its nature directly." Irrespective of whether or not one agrees with the position that there are obstructions to omniscience in the form of manifest consciousness, as long as one has not purified the misapprehension of holding the two truths as separate entities, there is no possibility of achieving complete enlightenment. Scholars differ as to the identity of this obscuration: some accept it as a type of consciousness, but others explain it in terms of the residual imprints alone and not a conscious state of mind. Achievement of enlightenment is constituted by the complete abandonment of that misapprehension. And in order to achieve such a state one has to have a complete development of the wisdom realizing emptiness. In order to advance emptiness realization, it is necessary to purify the negativities and accumulate merit. These are actually the two activities that dharma practitioners have to undertake.

To elaborate slightly, we can talk of three activities: accumulation of merit, purification of the negativities, and increasing one's own merit by rejoicing. When these are further elaborated, there is the seven-limbed practice, including requesting the teachings and supplicating the gurus to not enter nirvana, as discussed below. If one reads the root sutras of the *Abhisamayalankara* (Ornament of Clear Realizations) such as the *Eight Thousand Verse Prajnaparamita*, in the section on the path of meditation, there are very extensive explanations on rejoicing, dedication and so forth.

If you wish to perform the offering of ablution, it should be done at this point. Visualize the pavilion of ablution in a beautiful garden, as pleasant as possible, just as described in the *Jorchoe* practices, then invite the beings of the merit field. If you are engaging in an exclusively sutra practice, you perform the ablution while visualizing yourself in the form of a bikkshu. Offer the ablution to those who have assumed the form of detachment (that is, those in the form of bikkshus), with oneself in the form of a bikkshu, and to tantric deities with oneself in the form of a deity who is emanating goddesses who offer the ablution. After performing the ablution, visualize that the beings of the merit field return back to their places in the merit field. The ablution waters flow down to the six realms and relieve the specific sufferings of these realms: the waters become cooling nectar for the hot hell realms; warming nectar for the cold hell realms; illuminating wisdom for the animals; a relief from hunger and thirst in the hungry ghost realm, and so forth. Imagine that all these waters, in the nature of nectar and rays of light, satisfy and please the beings in the six realms. Although you may be practicing on an imagination level at the moment, through constant familiarity you will be able actually to bring about such a result in the future.

Lama Tsongkhapa said that since, during the generation stage, one arises from emptiness into the deity on the imagination level, there should be a state where in reality one can actually arise from emptiness into the deity. This is an obvious reference to the illusory body. In the same way, since we are working towards attaining a state where we can help sentient beings, we must train ourselves in such activities right from the beginning of the path, even if only through imagination. Transformation of the mind is only brought about through constant familiarity. But we should also undertake what is practically possible, and not leave everything at the imaginary level alone. When we read the collected works of many lamas we find a lot of techniques for the prolongation of life; we work on the prolongation of life, increase of wealth, and so forth mostly on the level of visualization, which, I feel, is the reason these techniques have not helped much. We have been a bit too idealistic by doing everything at an imagination level! Sometimes I think the Chinese are smarter in that respect! Both in religious practice and worldly life one has to be very realistic. I am not sure that someone having a very strong force of concentration can help others directly in a physical way; if such were the case, the many buddhas, who have very strong concentration, should have been able to help us a long time back! I think too much emphasis has been placed on visualization techniques for the prolongation of life and increase of wealth and so forth. Sometimes I feel that we lost our country because of having such attitudes. The country which was formerly well known as Tibet has now come to a point of disintegration. No-one took any special notice that the country was being gradually encroached on from its frontiers. So, just as it is sensible for all countries to learn from history and be more prepared for future events, so we should learn from our past experiences. Although we should put emphasis on meditative concentration and so on, yet if there is anything we can do on the practical side, we should also do that as long as it does not accumulate non-virtues.

Although we visualize that the nectars flow down to the beings of the six realms, relieving them of their specific sufferings, we should not be content with that, but when we actually see sentient beings suffering in reality, like those who are in the water and trying to get out, we should help them. Helping other sentient beings should not be kept just on the visualization level. When we sit down on our cushions we visualize all the sentient beings as our mothers, we focus on their welfare and even feel moved to tears, but when we end the session we fight with our neighbors and so forth. That is wrong. During our meditations we place all sentient beings in the state of buddhas, so that when we arise from the session we should help them as much as possible. If we cannot do this, at least we should not harm them. This, I think, is very important and is a very practical approach too.

I. PROSTRATION

The first of the seven-limbed practices is prostration. If you can actually prostrate it is good, otherwise you should just touch palms. It is also said that since one is undertaking the practice in connection with Yamantaka and one is in the form of simple Yamantaka, one face and two arms, one should imagine that all the bodies one has taken in innumerable past lifetimes arise in the form of as many Yamantakas as possible, and at the pores of these Yamantakas are many more Yamantakas; then prostrate with that visualization.

18. YOU WHOSE COMPASSION GRANTS EVEN THE
    SPHERE OF GREAT BLISS,
    THE SUPREME STATE OF THE THREE BODIES,

IN AN INSTANT,
O GURU WITH A JEWEL-LIKE BODY, VAJ-
RADHARA:
AT YOUR LOTUS FEET I PROSTRATE.

This first verse of prostration is to the guru in his enjoyment
body form, and expresses his specific qualities. Through the
force of the guru's inspiration, the actualization of even ultimate aims such as the three bodies—not to mention the aim
of temporary happiness—is possible within one instant. "In
an instant" does not mean in an instantaneous moment, but
refers rather to the lifetime of this human form. Our lifespan
is like an instant in comparison with the beginningless duration of cyclic existence.

19. YOU ARE THE PRISTINE AWARENESS OF ALL IN-
     FINITE CONQUERORS
     APPEARING WITH SUPREME SKILLFUL MEANS
     IN ANY WAY THAT TAMES,
     SUCH AS MANIFESTING IN THE GUISE OF A
     SAFFRON-ROBED MONK:
     I PROSTRATE AT YOUR FEET, O HOLY SAVIOR.

Here one prostrates to the guru as the emanation body. The
stanza says: Although you assume many appropriate forms suit-
ing the different dispositions and interests of sentient beings,
here at present, in order to tame me, you have assumed this
saffron-clad bikkshu form. I prostrate to you who are the refuge and also the protector.

20. SOLE SOURCE OF BENEFIT AND BLISS WITH-
     OUT EXCEPTION;
     YOU ELIMINATED ALL FAULTS AND THEIR IM-
     PRINTS,
     AND ARE A TREASURY OF MYRIAD JEWEL-LIKE
     QUALITIES;
     I PROSTRATE AT YOUR FEET, O VENERABLE
     GURU.

This is prostration to the guru as the truth body. First the verse mentions the abandonments: You have achieved a state where the faults of the emotional afflictions along with their imprints are extinguished, and have achieved realizations which have great qualities and which are the source of fulfillment of all wishes. It continues: You have achieved such a state through the force of compassion; because of that you are the source of all happiness, hope and help for sentient beings; therefore I prostrate to you.

In one of the notes on the lamrim text of Trichen Tampa Rabgyay, the author explains the meaning of *jetsun lama: je* indicates the "chief" among ordinary beings, because he has achieved all the realizations of the lower scope; *tsun* (industrious) refers to the pure observance of morality, said to be in the context of practice of the middling scope because there morality is the main practice; *lama* means "unsurpassable," an obvious reference to the practice of bodhicitta. So *jetsun lama* (venerable guru) has this special meaning, encompassing the guru's realizations of all the paths of the three scopes.

21. YOU ARE OF THE NATURE OF ALL BUDDHAS,
    TEACHERS OF ALL, INCLUDING THE GODS;
    THE SOURCE OF THE EIGHTY-FOUR THOUSAND
       PURE DHARMAS,
    YOU TOWER ABOVE THE WHOLE HOST OF
       ARYAS:
    I PROSTRATE TO YOU, O BENEVOLENT GURUS.

Here one prostrates to the guru while seeing him as the embodiment of each of the Three Jewels. The guru's mind is regarded as the buddha, his speech as the dharma, and his body as the sangha because he is the chief among the spiritual community.

The main focus here is on Lama Lozang Thubwang Dorje Chang. While you are reciting these verses, you should reflect on the meaning of, and the qualities of Lama Lozang Thubwang Dorje Chang with deep faith and respect.

22. TO THE GURUS OF THE THREE TIMES AND TEN
     DIRECTIONS,
     THE THREE SUPREME JEWELS AND ALL WOR-
     THY OF HOMAGE,
     WITH FAITH, CONVICTION AND OCEANS OF
     LYRIC PRAISE,
     I PROSTRATE, MANIFESTING FORMS AS
     NUMEROUS AS THE ATOMS OF THE WORLD.

This passage is one of prostration to the guru through the force
of faith and aspiration—the prostration through the mind.
"Praise" refers to prostration firstly through speech by sing-
ing praises with melodious tunes, and secondly through physical expressions. It is explained that at this point one can visualize all the bodies of one's past lives in human forms and imagine
making physical prostrations. One should do this while focusing upon all the figures of the merit field. In the *Lamrim
Chenmo* it is explained that one can visualize many heads on
one's body, and as many tongues, and sing praises and so forth
in this manner. This, however, is not indispensable.

II. OFFERINGS

23. O SAVIORS, O VENERABLE GURUS, TOGETHER
     WITH YOUR ENTOURAGE,
     I PRESENT YOU WITH OCEANS OF CLOUDS OF
     VARIOUS OFFERINGS.

This section concerns making offerings. If you have actually
arranged offering substances like the first portions of your food
and so forth, those should be taken as the basis of your visualization. One has to purify or transform them; therefore, it seems
that one is not actually offering these substances themselves,
but rather the transformed aspect of them. Therefore, I think
that, at the beginners' stage, the yogi has to depend on the
substantial basis even with respect to offerings, but later when

he progresses on the path, he becomes less dependent on the basis. In order for substances to be suitable for offering they should be endowed with the three attributes as explained in chapter two.

Emanate offering goddesses from your heart who hold appropriate offering substances. Having made the offerings, they should be dissolved back into your heart. Another way is to emanate all the offering goddesses at one time and have them make all these offerings and then to dissolve all of them into your heart, leaving the five goddesses of the sense objects who are later dissolved into the appropriate body mandala deities. The first line mentions the objects to whom you are making the offerings and then the verse goes on to explain the process of offering, and the substances offered.

If you want to perform the practice in an extensive manner according to the tradition of Yongdzin Yeshe Gyaltsen, verse 23 and the first two lines of verse 32 are recited repeatedly, each time inserting one of the verses which mention the specific offering substances (24—31).

Everything Yongdzin Yeshe Gyaltsen wrote was very extensive. Changkya Rolpai Dorje once asked him three questions in connection with the practice of highest yoga tantra, and it is said that the replies he got from Yongdzin Yeshe Gyaltsen did not please him very much, because each answer was so elaborate! But Longdoel Lama Rinpoche was the opposite: all his writings were very concise. It is said that when authors write something, they reveal their own personalities. Longdoel Lama Rinpoche used to say that too many words will harm visualization, so his writings are very integrated and concise. Elaborating the offerings has its own significance, but doing them in a more condensed way has the advantage that one can spend more time on the important points. Sometimes one may have the determination at the beginning to do a sadhana very well and so start out doing it in a very elaborate way, but then when the important section comes one may feel exhausted and not do it properly! For example, for practitioners of lamrim or mahamudra more emphasis has to be placed on the later section of this text.

24. FROM EXPANSIVE WELL-FASHIONED VESSELS,
    RADIANT AND PRECIOUS,
    GENTLY FLOW FOUR STREAMS OF PURIFYING
    NECTARS.

Here the style and the order of the offerings are made according to the custom in India where it is rather hot; hence cool drinks and so forth are offered first.

25. BEAUTIFUL FLOWERS IN TREES, AS BLOSSOMS
    AND
    IN EXQUISITELY ARRANGED GARLANDS, FILL
    THE EARTH AND SKY.

When you offer the flowers, offer flower plants, then loose flowers and also flower garlands, beautifully arranged and pervading the entire space and ground.

26. DRIFTS OF LAZULI SMOKE FROM FRAGRANT
    INCENSE
    BILLOW IN BLUE CLOUDS IN THE HEAVENS.

The incense smoke is blue like lapis lazuli, and pervades the sky like clouds.

27. FROM SUNS AND MOONS, GLITTERING JEWELS
    AND SCORES OF FLAMING LAMPS,
    JOYFUL LIGHT DISPELS THE DARKNESS OF A
    THOUSAND MILLION BILLION WORLDS.

Because light comes from the sun and moon (irrespective of whether the moon has its own light or not), one can offer these as lights. Here the text talks about different world systems, so your visualization of light should be so bright that it has the capacity to dispel the darkness within all these millions of world systems.

28. VAST SEAS OF SCENTED WATERS, IMBUED
    WITH THE FRAGRANCES
    OF SAFFRON, SANDALWOOD AND CAMPHOR,
    SWIRL OUT TO THE HORIZONS.

Visualize perfumes of sandal and so on as vast as the ocean.

29. DELICACIES OF GODS AND MEN, DRINKS AND
    WHOLESOME FEASTS
    WITH INGREDIENTS OF A HUNDRED FLAVORS,
    AMASS A MOUNT MERU.

30. MUSIC FROM AN ENDLESS VARIETY OF VARI-
    OUS INSTRUMENTS
    BLENDS INTO A SYMPHONY FILLING THE
    THREE REALMS.

You should visualize different types of instruments, things like drums, cymbals and also modern musical instruments such as found in the West. You can emanate and offer whatever musical instruments you can imagine.

31. GODDESSES OF SENSE OBJECTS, HOLDING SYM-
    BOLS OF
    SIGHT, SOUND, SMELL, TASTE AND TOUCH,
    PERVADE ALL DIRECTIONS.

This is the offering of the five sense objects. This also refers to the inner objects as explained in the Guhyasamaja tantra. When you offer the external desire objects, you should emanate various offering goddesses who hold the particular hand symbols such as a mirror, cymbals for music and so forth. Having made the offerings, visualize these offering goddesses such as Rupavajras and Shabdavajras dissolving into the offering goddesses in the body mandala of the main central figure.

Through the force of dissolving them into the mandala deities, one gains a special power for inducing bliss. But for other types of offering substances, you emanate offering goddesses who, having made the offerings, should be dissolved into your heart. In one of Pelmang Kunchok Gyaltsen's commentaries, he said that in the context of the lower tantras it is not necessary to dissolve these offering goddesses back into the heart, but in the practice of the highest yoga tantra it is important.

32. TO YOU, O SAVIORS, TREASURES OF COM-
    PASSION,
    EMINENT AND SUPREME FIELD OF MERIT, I
    PRESENT WITH PURE FAITH:
    MOUNT MERU AND THE FOUR CONTINENTS A
    BILLION TIMES OVER,
    THE SEVEN PRECIOUS ROYAL EMBLEMS, THE
    PRECIOUS MINOR SYMBOLS AND MORE,
    PERFECTLY DELIGHTFUL ENVIRONMENTS
    AND BEINGS,
    AND A GREAT TREASURY OF ALL THAT GODS
    AND MEN USE OR DESIRE.

This is the mandala offering. If possible, you should say the long version of the mandala; if not, just follow the short version. There are different types of mandala offerings: the twenty-three heap mandala, the twenty-five heap mandala, to which is added twelve to become a thirty-seven heap mandala. Any of these can be offered. If you are offering mandalas repeatedly, I think you should offer the one of twenty-three heaps because it has a special inspirational power. The mandala offering also has different aspects, like internal, external and secret. The outer offering refers to the offering of the mandala of the universe system. The inner mandala refers to offering the parts of one's own body visualized in the form of the parts of the universe system. There is a verse for offering the parts of one's body as a mandala. There is the story of Naropa making an inner mandala offering to his master Tilopa. There is also a secret mandala offering: this refers to imagining the mandala offering as the manifestation of the wisdom of bliss and emptiness; and when it is further viewed as being in the nature of the very subtle wind and mind, it becomes the offering of the suchness mandala.

The universe system that we offer is explained in the texts, but that does not mean that the universe exists in such a way— even in the buddhist texts there are many different world systems explained. There are even different explanations regarding the size of the sun and moon. But these days we have facts which are established through scientific observation, and it is not necessary to stick literally to the presentations in the *Abhidharmakosha* (Treasury of Knowledge), as they contradict our direct perception. As long as one holds to a position which contradicts direct experience it cannot be regarded as well founded, because it is a buddhist principle that when we draw conclusions it has to be done through a logical process, finally leading to a direct experience, and no position should be held which contradicts experience. Lama Tsongkhapa, in the opening remarks of *Lekshe Nyingpo* (Essence of Elegant Exposition), [a treatise on the definitive and interpretive meanings of Buddha's words], said that a person who adheres to a position contradictory to logic cannot be taken as a valid master.

33. ON THE SHORE OF A WISH-GRANTING SEA
    GROW LOTUSES
    WHICH ARE OFFERINGS ARISEN FROM SAM-
    SARA'S AND NIRVANA'S VIRTUES;
    BOTH REAL AND EMANATED, THEY CAPTIVATE
    ALL HEARTS;
    FLOWERS, BEING BOTH WORLDLY AND SUPER-
    MUNDANE VIRTUES
    OF MY OWN AND OTHERS' THREE DOORS,
    BRIGHTEN ALL PLACES.
    THIS GARDEN IS DIFFUSED WITH MYRIAD
    FRAGRANCES   OF   SAMANTABHADRA
    OFFERINGS;

IT IS LADEN WITH FRUIT—THE THREE TRAIN-
INGS, TWO STAGES AND FIVE PATHS;
I OFFER THIS IN ORDER TO PLEASE YOU, O
VENERABLE GURUS.

This passage is the offering of one's own practice. It is written in a poetic form; one does the offering as described in the
verses. Visualize a very vast ocean of offerings, those actually
arranged and those mentally created, within which are all of
your offerings in the form of a very wide and extensive lotus.
Visualize the goodness and virtues included within worldly and
supermundane levels of all the world systems in the form of
a large lotus, and imagine all of your own virtues arising in
the form of lotuses too. Visualize the fifteen paths according
to sutrayana and also the specific paths of the tantras in the
form of a beautiful garden; these are offered to the guru. This
constitutes the offering of one's own practice.

34. I OFFER A DRINK OF CHINA TEA IN THE COLOR
OF SAFFRON,
RICH IN A HUNDRED FLAVORS, WITH A DELI-
CATE BOUQUET;
THE FIVE HOOKS, FIVE LAMPS AND SO FORTH
ARE PURIFIED, TRANSFORMED, AND IN-
CREASED INTO A SEA OF NECTAR.

This is the offering of tea. There is one tradition that says it
is an inner offering, and another classified it as an outer offering. I think there is a special significance to it being a sort
of indigenous Tibetan offering. But if tea is strong it causes
high blood pressure, and if it is too greasy it causes jaundice!
Atisha praised Tibetan tea, but these days it is actually caus-
ing a lot of troubles. As I have remarked before, those who
make offerings to the three monastic universities in South India should concentrate more on making offerings of food and
not of tea. Many doctors have told me that Tibetan tea causes
a lot of illnesses. In Tibet it may have been helpful because

of the climate and so forth, but here in India, which is a hot country, I think it is quite wrong to overindulge in it. So it is better to concentrate on making offerings of food like fruits, vegetables and so on to the spiritual communities.

I will now make a remark. Putting too much emphasis on making thanksgiving offerings for the geshe exams is actually quite wrong. If it is only the offerings one makes that matter then someone having no knowledge but enough funds would easily be able to become a geshe. One should put more emphasis on the actual geshe studies. I had to write to the monastic universities pointing out that, during some geshe examinations, I noticed that one among the group replies to debate questions while his companions just keep quiet and look very majestic, which is not good. This is not very fair, because those who have studied get the title, and those who have not studied properly also get the title. As we say in Tibet, "A *karma-nga* (a Tibetan coin) for a yak's head and a *karma-nga* for a goat's head!" Just having the title *geshe* does not serve much purpose! So, putting too much emphasis on the geshe offering (to be made by the candidates) is not very good. One should put more emphasis on study, and demonstrate one's scholarship by replying during the examination.

I think it is very important to take great care of our food. When I was in South India I especially took note and found that Gyudmed Tantric College has the best food! Daily food in Gaden Shartse, Jhangtse and at Drepung was not good. It is widely said in Tibet, "Request a person to pray like a tantric college monk and also eat like a tantric college monk!" This tradition has been maintained, I found! So, taking very strong tea is very harmful. If the geshes drink too much Tibetan tea and it causes them to die prematurely, I really feel a great sense of loss, because it takes so much effort and many years to produce a geshe. If having made the effort, the geshe then wastes it through his own carelessness about food, it is really a very sad thing. So, taking this very strong tea and so on, and also not being very careful of hygiene and not seeking medication when one is ill, is very wrong. One sick monk came from Mondgod recently and requested me to make prayers—that is actually too late. One should be careful right from the beginning.

For the lay person, smoking cigarettes is also harmful to the health. Although it is not against the law, and everyone has a choice, that it is harmful is generally accepted in the world. Once, Kyabje Ling Rinpoche told me that when he went to the West for medical treatment, he was told that being too fat is not very good, but that all the doctors who said that were themselves very fat! It is the Westerners who say that cigarette smoking is very harmful, but they are the ones who promote cigarettes through extensive advertising, and they themselves smoke. They put so much emphasis on material development, hardly having the time to eat, but now they are the ones complaining about the side effects of material progress, such as pollution and the destruction of the environment and so forth. I can understand that for those in Tibet, because the situation was so sad, smoking might have helped by giving temporary comfort, but because in reality it harms the body it is not good. Similarly, snuff is also very bad. There are a few exceptions where people have various illnesses. Even Padmasambhava talked a lot, in one of his prophecies, about the negative effects of taking tobacco. Gungtang Rinpoche expressed the same view. So, with these types of addictive substances one should be careful right from the beginning. Once one has become addicted, these substances might actually cause one to be more unhealthy, even after one gives them up.

The "five hooks" and "five lamps" refer to the five meats and the five nectars, "hooks" indicating that the siddhis (powerful attainments) are hooked in, and "lamps," that they are illuminated. The five lamps are the ripening factors for the illusory body, and in that way dispel the darkness of sentient beings. This is called an inner offering. In the practice of highest yoga tantra, inner offering is very important, and practitioners are recommended to keep a vajra and bell and also an inner offering which should be hidden from other persons' sight, even if it is merely a drawing. The inner offering is made after having made the outer offerings. This offering is *inner* because the substances that you are offering here are substances possessed by a living being within his body. This inner offering is being made to the root and lineage gurus, meditational deities, and so forth, and also to the local spirits. You should also taste it yourself.

35. I OFFER EVEN ILLUSION-LIKE CONSORTS, OF
    YOUTHFUL SPLENDOR,
    SLENDER AND SKILLED IN THE SIXTY-FOUR
    ARTS OF LOVE;
    A HOST OF MESSENGER DANKINIS—
    FIELD-BORN, MANTRA-BORN AND SIMULTANE-
    OUSLY BORN.

This is the secret offering. The verse talks of different types of consorts, as found in the *Kachem Lung Kurma*. What is meant by "field-born" is those who are physically dwelling in the twenty-four places; "mantra-born" refers to the ones who have achieved the generation stage; and "simultaneously born" refers to those who have achieved the realizations from the meaning clear light of the completion stage onwards. According to the *Great Exposition of Tantra*, there is another interpretation: "field-born" refers to the consorts who have achieved the realization of the generation stage; "mantra-born" to those on the completion stage of the three isolations and illusory body; and "simultaneously born" to those on the stages from meaning clear light onwards. "Messenger" means those consorts who assist progress on the path. When you make the secret offering, you emanate many consorts, who should not be visualized as embracing the main figure but should rather dissolve into the consort of Vajradhara at the heart of Lama Lozang Thubwang Dorje. Imagine Vajradhara and the central figure experiencing great bliss.

36. I OFFER YOU THE GREAT WISDOM OF CO-
    EMERGENT BLISS, UNOBSTRUCTED,

THE SPHERE OF THE TRUE, UNELABORATED
NATURE OF ALL PHENOMENA...
BEYOND THOUGHT AND EXPRESSION, SPON-
TANEOUS AND INSEPARABLE, THE SUPREME
ULTIMATE BODHICITTA.

This is the offering of suchness. Through the force of entering into union with such a consort, you experience a wisdom
which is free of obscurations and experience a simultaneous
bliss which is inseparable from emptiness, the nature of
phenomena. "Inseparability" here is not used in the sense
of inseparability of the object and its quality, emptiness—this
would not help to free one from samsara. But what helps the
practitioner to eliminate his obstructions is when he unites inseparably the subjective wisdom of simultaneous bliss realizing emptiness with the total absence of dualistic appearance
of subject and object.

The last two lines and verse 52 are very similar to the ter-
minology found in the writings on the dzogchen (great perfection) school. When the treatises of the great perfection school
talk about the *kadag* (purity) and *lhundrup* (spontaneity), they
talk in terms of the inseparability of the two. If we take the
meaning of this inseparability only in terms of the spontaneity
being in the nature of purity or emptiness as some writings
do, then the meaning may not be profound. But if we understand it in terms of inseparability of the subject and object
in terms of the subject being absorbed in the object, the explanations of the Gelug school would help you better understand the dzogchen view of purity and spontaneity.

What is meant by *spontaneity?* Gungtang Rinpoche said one
should understand it as *union.* How is that? Because on the
basis of being the wisdom of inseparability of bliss and emptiness it has the full potential to arise into many different emanations. This is possible because of the "mount" wind of that
wisdom mind. Such a subtle wind becomes manifest when one
realizes that wisdom and the illusory body are the sport of the
mere wind and the mind. Spontaneity is referred to as union,

on the basis of that understanding. So, the ultimate truth, the wisdom of bliss and emptiness, is regarded as one part of a pair, and the conventional truth, which here refers to the illusory body, as the other part; and the integration of these two into one unified form is what is meant by spontaneity or union. Such a state is inexpressible and is also inconceivable.

The inseparability of the two truths is regarded as superior to the inseparability of bliss and emptiness. The original Sanskrit term for "ultimate" is *paramatha* which also has the connotation of supreme. Gungtang Rinpoche said that there the reference is to the latter. So, in the context of highest yoga tantra, the *paramatha sattya*, or the ultimate truth, is the clear light. When we talk of spontaneity, I think the understanding of the dzogchen interpretation is quite helpful. *Kadag*, or purity, refers to the ultimate nature as expounded by Buddha in the second turning of the wheel. The understanding of spontaneity has to be developed on the basis of the fundamental innate mind of clear light. So I think the interpretation of spontaneity as union has a close connection to the treatises of the perfection school—that is my own personal observation. I do not know whether it is a fact or not. Just as is explained in Aryadeva's *Chatu-Shataka Shastra*, the impartial trainees who have intelligence should analyze for themselves. Therefore, you must analyze for yourselves.

At this point it is necessary to have an understanding of union, and the object to whom you are making this offering should be seen as having actualized the resultant union state. Also, the substances that you are offering should be viewed as the sport, or manifestation, of the mere wind and mind.

The outer offerings are associated with the vase initiation, the inner offerings with the secret initiation, the secret offerings with the wisdom-knowledge initiation, and the offering of suchness with the word initiation. If you have an understanding of the suchness offering only on the basis of the inseparability of bliss and emptiness, it is not complete. You have to understand it on the basis of the union of the two truths; then it constitutes the suchness offering as related to the fourth initiation. You can find the explanation of the offering of suchness associated with the word initiation in the writings of Akhu Sherab Gyatso and Gungtang Rinpoche. It is not very explicit in other works. This is a very important topic.

37. I OFFER ALL TYPES OF POTENT MEDICINES TO CURE THE FOUR HUNDRED AFFLICTIONS CAUSED BY DEFILEMENTS...

This is the offering of medicine. It is said that if the practitioner can offer the medicines appropriate to his own illness it will help his health.

> ...AND I OFFER MYSELF AS A SERVANT TO PLEASE YOU:
> PRAY KEEP ME IN YOUR SERVICE AS LONG AS SPACE ENDURES.

These two lines are also found in the *Bodhisattvacharyavatara*. Of all the offerings that you made earlier—both those owned by you and those not owned—although those mentally created serve as a cause for being able to make offerings in the future, the physical body that you have now is something that you can offer in reality. You should not make these offerings in order to have happiness for yourself, but rather to please Lama Lozang Thubwang Dorje Chang, who is engaged in the activity of helping sentient beings infinite as space: In order to please you, I offer myself to serve you. Requesting him to take you as his servant is very important. There is a tradition when making offerings that one asks to be placed within the guru's meditated protection circle.

This concludes the offering limb.

III. CONFESSION

38. BEFORE THOSE HAVING GREAT COMPASSION,
    I CONFESS WITH REGRET, AND VOW NEVER TO
    REPEAT,
    WHATEVER NON-VIRTUOUS AND EVIL ACTIONS
    I HAVE DONE SINCE BEGINNINGLESS TIME,
    CAUSED OTHERS TO DO, OR IN WHICH I HAVE
    REJOICED.

This is the limb of confession, or disclosure. For us beginners, at the initial stage there is a possibility that we can refrain from indulging in negative actions in the future, but if
there is no process by which we can purify negativities committed in the past, there is not much hope. However, there
is such a process.

If you do not probe deeply, you may feel that you have not
committed any grave negative actions, but if you examine the
state of your mind, you will find that such emotional factors
as hatred, attachment and so forth arise very easily, even though
there are hardly any external circumstances to justify them.
This is possible chiefly because you are habituated to the negative states of mind, and through their force you are also used
to indulging in negative actions. That is a clear indication of
your long-time familiarity with the negative states of mind
which impel you to indulge in both physical and verbal negative actions. So, this proves that you actually do have a very
great accumulation of negativities from the past. Those must
be purified with a very strong force of regret from the depths
of your heart.

If you wish to undertake this practice of purification in relation to Vajrasattva, you can visualize a Vajrasattva emanating from the heart of the central figure and sitting above your
crown while you do the Vajrasattva mantra recitation. Or, you
can visualize a Vajrasattva emanating from the heart of the Vajrasattva lord and consort which are among the deities of highest
yoga tantra; he sits above your crown while you do the purifi-

cation practice. Or, at this point you can do the separate Vajrasattva meditation by generating into the deity. Regarding the
process of purification, you could do a visualization such as
the downward, upward, and instant driving out of the negativities. You can also perform the visualization of receiving the
four initiations, which can be done in conjunction with the
hundred-syllable mantra recitation. At the end, the Vajrasattva
above your crown should be dissolved into yourself. Then cultivate the strong determination never to indulge in those negative actions again, by reciting the verse:

> Due to my ignorance of the proper actions,
> I have transgressed and degenerated my commitments;
> O, guru, be my lord and protect me.
> I take refuge in you, the foremost vajra-holder,
> The embodiment of great compassion,
> And the lord of all beings.

If you are emphasizing the practice of purification, at this
point it is very good to perform prostrations while reciting the
thirty-five confessional buddhas' names. The thirty-five confessional buddhas whom you have visualized in the merit field
could be visualized coming nearer and surrounding the root
guru. While focusing on them unwaveringly, prostrate and recite their names. Pelmang Koenchog Gyaltsen said that while
one is reciting the confessional buddhas' names, it is good to
visualize all the negativities gathered at the tip of one's tongue
as a black heap. In Gyaltsab Je's commentary on *Tung Shak*
(The Confessional Buddhas' Sutra), the author mentions that
uttering the names of the individual buddhas purifies the negative actions committed over a certain number of eons. This
claim must have some sutra as a source, for he would not say
this without an authentic reference. Since the mere utterance
of the names has such great power, and since it is the tongue
which produces the sound, I think it is very appropriate to
visualize the negativities at the tip of the tongue and imagine
them being purified due to the recitations. If you are repeating the prostrations many times, it is very good to keep on

repeating the names of the confessional buddhas. Otherwise, at this point you could recite *Tung Shak* in its entirety, and at the points where one says "I prostrate," join your two palms.

A proper confession requires the four powers: (1) the power of the basis; (2) the power of repentance; (3) the power of the actual antidote; and (4) the resolve never to indulge in the actions again. As the great yogi Milarepa said:

> When I investigated if confession could purify the negativities,
> I found that it is repentance which cleanses them.

The force of repentance is the most important of the powers. You have to really regret the negative actions committed, from the depths of your heart. We have committed many negativities in our past lives and even in this lifetime. Kyabje Trijang Rinpoche used to say that the force behind our negative actions is irresistible, like a falling boulder, and the force behind our virtuous actions is just like leading a donkey uphill. This is very true. Our practice of virtue in this lifetime is really very weak, but the negative actions are very strong and complete in all aspects—the motives, the preparations, and the actual acts themselves. Even for those weak virtues that we do accumulate, there are many obstacles. In addition, because we have very strong faith and interest in the dharma, we try to grab at the highest teachings without considering our own abilities; there is a danger of actually committing negativities even in that way. Therefore, we must have committed all sorts of negativities out of our naturally ignorant tendencies.

Just as explained in the *Bodhisattvacharyavatara*, although we resolve that we shall purify all sentient beings' negativities and their imprints, we still let ourselves come under the influence of negative actions and continue to indulge in them. This is really sad. The method for purifying all the past actions is the practice of confession. Therefore, at this juncture, as you know how to purify and have the capacity to do so owing to the kindness of the guru, you should engage in the practice of confession, which will make you feel free and relieved at the end. And then, being mindful of the great qualities of the body, speech and mind of the buddhas, you should generate the intention: I shall never hide from you all the negativities that I have committed, but rather, disclose them and purify them. Although there may be certain types of negativities which you are prone to committing, nevertheless it is very important at this point to resolve that you shall never indulge in them again, even at the cost of your life. It is said that although they might be easily committed again, resolving thus does not constitute lying. This strong resolve is very important, as it helps to purify the negativities. At this point you can also perform the Samayavajra meditation.

IV. REJOICING

39. THOUGH ALL THINGS ARE LIKE A DREAM,
    LACKING INHERENT EXISTENCE,
    I SINCERELY REJOICE IN EVERY VIRTUE THAT
    EVER ARISES
    AS THE HAPPINESS AND JOY OF ALL ARYAS
    AND ORDINARY BEINGS.

This is the limb of rejoicing. Here you should admire and rejoice in the accumulation of virtues not only of yourself, but also of other sentient beings, buddhas, arhats, and so forth. You must admire and cultivate joy from the depths of your heart for your own virtues, too. Your attitude towards the virtues of others should not be influenced by jealousy. So, at this point, reflect upon the great qualities of the figures of the merit field and then rejoice in them. Here the text says, "Although all phenomena lack any status apart from nominal existence on the conventional level, yet since positive fruits are produced from positive causes, I shall rejoice in the deeds of others."

V. REQUEST TO TURN THE WHEEL OF DHARMA

40. SHOWER RAINS OF VAST AND PROFOUND
    DHARMA, I PRAY,
    FROM A GATHERING OF A MILLION CLOUDS OF
    PERFECT WISDOM AND COMPASSION,
    TO GROW, SUSTAIN, AND PROPAGATE A GARDEN
    OF MOON FLOWERS
    OF BENEFIT AND BLISS FOR THE LIMITLESS
    BEINGS.

This verse requests the guru to turn the wheel of dharma. Here you reflect on the great qualities of the omniscient mind of the guru-Vajradhara. It says, ''From the infinite space of your compassionate mind, in order to generate and increase the realizations in myself and other sentient beings, please shower down the rain of profound and vast teachings.'' At this point you could visualize offering a dharmachakra (dharma wheel) or a conch to the central figure. Imagine that the figures of the merit field consent to your request and are very pleased.

VI. ENTREATING NOT TO ENTER INTO NIRVANA

41. THOUGH YOUR VAJRA BODY IS SUBJECT TO NEI-
    THER BIRTH NOR DEATH,
    BUT IS A VESSEL OF THE MIGHTY KING, UNIFI-
    CATION,
    PLEASE ABIDE FOREVER ACCORDING TO MY
    WISHES,
    NOT PASSING BEYOND SORROW UNTIL THE
    END OF SAMSARA.

This is the verse of supplicating the merit field figures not to enter into nirvana. Generally, *vajra body* refers to the illusory bodies both of and beyond the state of impure illusory body; but it also means the state which is the fulfillment of the abandonments and the realizations. Here it says, "Although you have achieved the truth body and therefore are beyond the state of death, you have assumed a form which is visible and accessible to us ordinary beings." So, we are requesting this form not to enter into nirvana. At this point imagine offering a precious throne with two crossed vajras.

VII. DEDICATION

42. I DEDICATE THE COLLECTION OF WHITE VIR-
     TUES THUS CREATED
     TO SENTIENT BEINGS THAT THEY MAY BE IN-
     SEPARABLY CARED FOR IN ALL FUTURE
     LIVES
     BY VENERABLE GURUS KIND IN THE THREE
     WAYS,
     AND MAY ATTAIN THE VAJRADHARA UNIFI-
     CATION.

Now comes the limb of dedication. Focus on all the virtues that you have accumulated by having visualized the merit field and engaged in the practices of prostration, purification and so forth, and in all other virtuous actions. Dedicate these merits to all sentient beings, including yourself, so that they may be taken care of by the guru throughout all lifetimes. Thus the merits will not be exhausted by simply producing insignificant fruits. This should be done with a strong force of aspiration.

With this practice, the accumulation of merit by meditating upon the field of merit is concluded.

5 Praise and Requests

Request prayers follow the seven-limbed practice. I think that the actual practice or main emphasis of guru devotion starts here. To make the request prayers with faith and respect, first reflect on the advantages of properly relying on a guru and the disadvantages of not relying properly and of having a breach in guru devotion practice. Reflecting on the qualities of the master, cultivate faith. Guru yoga is not just a practice where one visualizes a deity and then makes offerings of the seven limbs, but rather it is one where one views one's own root guru as a real buddha from the depths of one's heart. Having cultivated that view and attitude and the necessary strong faith, one then engages in the practice of actually pleasing the guru by following his advice, and it is through such a practice that one should try to have a transference of the guru's realizations to one's own mental continuum. Such a practice is called guru yoga.

As it says in Tsongkhapa's "Songs of Spiritual Experience":

The root from which all possible good collections
duly result during this and future lives,
is the dutiful and effortless reliance in thought and deed
on one's holy master who reveals the path.

Seeing this, please him by the offering of practicing as he
  says,
Not giving up even at the cost of your life.
I, a yogin, have practiced like this,
You who also seek liberation please practice likewise.

If one relies on the guidance of a guru, one comes closer
to the achievement of buddhahood, and accumulates the same
merits as one would gain from making offerings to all the
buddhas. So, reflect upon these advantages. In short, if we
look carefully and probe deeper, we will find that (i) even the
slightest pleasures that we experience during this lifetime are
generally the results of our virtuous actions in the past; (ii)
these virtues depend on circumstances for their arisal; and (iii)
there is no way that negative actions could produce happiness.
Because of the activities of the guru, at this juncture in this
lifetime we have a great opportunity. As this is the case, there
is no question that the achievement of realizations and the attainment of the resultant state are definitely dependent upon
proper reliance on the guru. This shows that temporary and
also ultimate happiness are the result of proper reliance on the
guru. In this life, we have actually met with the spiritual guru;
so, having reflected on the advantages of proper reliance on
him, you should convince yourself and decide that you will
relate to him in the proper manner, and rejoice in the fact that
you have not made any mistake in seeking a guru.

Merely having a relationship with a guru does not help; it
is necessary to have proper reliance, because if there is a breach
in guru devotion it is very dangerous. That there are great disadvantages and bad consequences has been explained both in
the sutras and tantras. If, for example, one were to speak of
faults of the guru or insult the guru, because he is the source
through which all the activities of the buddhas reach us, indirectly one would be insulting all the buddhas. So, if one were
to have a breach in one's guru devotion it would hinder one's
practices even in this lifetime, not to mention one's future fate.
Therefore just seeking a guru is not sufficient; one has to un-

dertake a proper reliance on him, modelled on that of such practitioners as Naropa. Reflect on the biographies of the masters of the past who are the examples for guru devotion practice. We can see practitioners who, at the mention of their root guru's name, actually have tears come into their eyes— these should be taken as the model. Then make the determination: I shall maintain my guru devotion practice properly. The disadvantages of not properly relying on the guru are the reverse of the advantages: for example, not achieving one's ultimate aims. All temporary and ultimate goodness is the consequence of relying on the guru, and all suffering and unsatisfactoriness is the consequence of not meeting a guru or not properly relying on him.

Next you should reflect on the fact that you have been so fortunate to have met such a spiritual master. At this point, although one has visualized a central figure in the form of Lama Tsongkhapa, in order to create a greater effect on the mind it is recommended that one visualize and focus more attention on the root guru in front. And it is even recommended that one should visualize him not only in his ordinary appearance but also with all the seeming defects or superficial faults that one sees. Then reflect on the reasons that prove the guru to be a buddha, thinking of how he is the performer of the activities for the buddhas, and so forth. If you think about it, the little understanding of the dharma that you have was not cultivated just on your own, through your own intelligence or wisdom or smartness, or because of having a good family background, but rather it is the product of the guru's kindness. You can imagine what your fate would have been if you had not met with an experienced spiritual master, even though you might have very great intelligence and be very sharp. Rejoice in the fact that you have such a great opportunity.

When the buddhas cultivated bodhicitta, they took us into the sphere of their compassion and their aspiration to attain complete enlightenment, so we are included within their bodhicitta. To take the example of Buddha Shakyamuni, with whom we have closer ties than with other buddhas, although we do not see him with our naked eyes, it is definite that he is engaged in the activity of helping us. If such is the case, there is no way for him to do it apart from through the medium of our spiritual gurus. This proves that the guru is the performer of the actions of the Buddha. How can he be the Buddha, you might wonder, if he has such and such defects and faults? To answer such a doubt, you should consider your own opinion of yourself: Even though you may have many negativities and faults, you may still have a perfect image of yourself. We see a lot of cases where people are really very bad but they think the world of themselves! So, it is questionable whether the faults and defects actually exist within the guru or whether they are merely projections of your deluded mind. You can conclude that the faults you see in your spiritual guru are your projection.

From another perspective, you could consider that the showing of such faults by the guru is actually a great kindness, because it is through his appearing in such an ordinary way that you have access to his kindness and can see him and listen to his words. His assuming such an ordinary form is not done because of inability, but rather because such a form is appropriate to your own faculties. If the Buddha remained in the truth body he would be directly perceptible only by the buddhas themselves; if he assumed the enjoyment body it would be accessible only to the arya bodhisattvas of high levels; and if he assumed the supreme emanation body it would be accessible only to beings of high faculties. Since we are not in any of these categories, we can conclude that his assuming such an ordinary form is through the force of his kindness to us. This also shows his skillful means.

Assuming an ordinary appearance does not mean just being devoid of a crown protrusion or wisdom eye and so on, but rather, it means actually appearing as just an ordinary person. One cannot distinguish between an ordinary being and an arya, or noble being, from the mere physical appearance. Rather, the distinction is made on the level of realization—whether the person has realized emptiness directly or not. In the same way, whether or not a person is a bodhisattva is determined on the basis of whether or not he has generated bodhicitta. All these distinctions have to be made on the basis of the level of mind. In the same way, what is meant by assuming an ordinary form is: having all the normal human faults, like emotional afflictions and so on. A person appearing to be free of these faults is generally regarded as uncommon, even in conventional terms. So, all the activities which show that the guru possesses negative states of mind are actually skillful means. It is because of these means that we can see him and have access to his wisdom. If he had not assumed this form there is no way he could tame us. To give an example: If we want to call a kitten we have to imitate the mother cat by calling "miaow!" so as to suit its mind. You can hide and call the kitten to you by imitating that sound. If, on the other hand you were to recite a text or something like that, the kitten might run away! In the same way, if the guru had not assumed the ordinary form, but his ultimate form of the truth body, he would not be accessible to us. Therefore, thinking along such lines, and seeing superficial faults in gurus as an expression of skillful means should help your faith increase. Through such techniques you can actually cause the perception of faults in the guru to assist the increase of faith in him. So, with such reflections you should repeat the name praise verse of Lama Tsongkhapa, thinking: Due to your kindness I have gained such opportunities; if I had not been taken into your care what would my fate be? Done in this way, your repetition of the Lama Tsongkhapa praise verse would be very effective.

There are many different versions of "Migtsema," the praise verse of Lama Tsongkhapa—one having five lines, one having four, one with six, one with nine and so forth. The praise verse to Lama Tsongkhapa to be recited here is the one with nine lines. Many techniques related to this "Migtsema" have been explained. It is said that the four-line and five-line "Migtsemas" are to be recited during Gaden Lhagyama guru yoga, and the nine-line praise verse of Lama Tsongkhapa in connection with *Lama Choepa*. But in some commentaries, it is mentioned that here in *Lama Choepa* the four- and five-line verses are sufficient.

The nine-line version is:

> Vajradhara, source of all realizations, lord of sages;
> Avalokiteshvara, great treasure of compassion of non-apprehension
> Manjushri, lord of stainless wisdom;
> Lord of the secret, destroying all lords of maras;
> Sumatikirti, crown jewel of the sages of the land of snows:
> To you, guru-buddha, comprising the three objects of refuge,
> I make requests, showing respect with my three doors.
> Please grant your blessings to ripen and liberate myself and others;
> Please bestow the supreme and common realizations.

If you are practicing lamrim you could recite the request to the lineage gurus of lamrim before reciting the praise verse of Lama Tsongkhapa, or if you are undertaking this practice in connection with mahamudra, you could recite the prayer to the lineage gurus of mahamudra here.

Sometimes, for the sake of the general welfare of Tibet, you may like to make special prayers to Guru Padmasambhava and repeat his mantra at this point. This is also very good. Just as Gedun Gyatso, the Second Dalai Lama, said:

> Padmasambhava, who is the chief among all the realized beings,
> Atisha, who is the chief of all the scholars,
> and Manjushri Lama Tsongkhapa—
> All of them are of the one nature and also manifestations of each other.

So, at this point you could make requesting prayers to Guru Padmasambhava. It is very good if you can make the requesting prayers on the basis of an exclusively Nyingma text; if not, you can do it in connection with *Lama Choepa*. Generally, I repeat the mantra of Guru Padmasambhava right after the name verse of Lama Tsongkhapa.

Next comes the making of requesting prayers to the guru, while reflecting on his qualities.

43. YOU ARE A SOURCE OF VIRTUE, AN IMMENSE OCEAN OF MORAL DISCIPLINE, AND BRIM WITH A TREASURY OF THE JEWELS OF VAST LEARNING; MASTER, SECOND KING OF SAGES CLAD IN SAFFRON, O ELDER, HOLDER OF VINAYA, I MAKE REQUESTS TO YOU.

This sequence of verses concerns cultivating faith by reflecting upon the guru's qualities, and cultivating respect by reflecting upon his kindness. The first passage outlines the way in which one cultivates faith. Just as Sakyaprabha said in his *Three Hundred Stanzas on Vinaya*:

Perfect in morality and well versed in vinaya,
He who has compassion towards the sick and has noble
  companions
Strives to help others through both material and spiritual
  gifts
And is capable of giving advice at the right time—
Such a being can be hailed as a qualified teacher.

Reflect upon the fact that the guru is endowed with the qualifications as outlined in the vinaya texts, as it is on the basis of morality that one has to achieve the realizations of concentration and wisdom, the two subsequent trainings. Morality is here likened to a vast ocean. Even if one has pure morality, if one's learning is not great, one will not be able to guide skillfully. Therefore, the guru should be knowledgeable in the practice of morality. One should reflect on the fact that the guru is endowed with the qualifications as explained in the vinaya, is a bikkshu and is like the successor of Buddha, and on that basis cultivate faith.

44. YOU HAVE THE TEN QUALITIES THAT MAKE
ONE A SUITABLE GUIDE
TO TEACH THE PATH OF THOSE-GONE-TO-BLISS;
LORD OF DHARMA, REPRESENTING ALL THE
CONQUERORS,
O MAHAYANA GURU, I MAKE REQUESTS TO YOU.

The second stanza alludes to the guru possessing the ten qualifications[27] as outlined in the sutras. These qualifications of a perfect teacher are set down by Asanga in his *Mahayana-Sutralankara* (Ornament of Mahayana Sutras).

45. WITH YOUR THREE DOORS WELL-SUBDUED,
WISE, PATIENT AND HONEST,
HONORABLE, KNOWING THE TANTRAS AND
RITUALS,
HAVING BOTH SETS OF TEN PRINCIPLES,
SKILLED IN DRAWING AND TEACHING,
O FOREMOST VAJRA-HOLDER, I MAKE RE-
QUESTS TO YOU.

Below is an abbreviation of a stanza from *Guru Panchasika* which outlines the qualifications of the guru: "He should have full expertise in both ten fields, skill in the drawing of mandalas, full knowledge of how to explain the tantra, supreme pure faith and his senses fully under control." "Knowing the tantras and rituals" means that he has the knowledge of how to employ the concentrations, mantras and so forth. Then it speaks of the two sets of ten principles.[28]

Stanzas 43-45 speak of the qualifications of the guru as explained in the vinaya, sutra and tantra. If your guru is a fully ordained bikkshu, these meditations are very appropriate. So, reflecting on these qualifications, you should make requesting prayers (*sol deb*) from the depths of your heart. *Sol deb* has the connotation of requesting and receiving inspirations; that is the meaning of requesting prayers.

46. YOU UNMISTAKENLY SHOW THE GOOD WAY OF
    THOSE-GONE-TO-BLISS
    TO THE UNRULY MIGRATORS UNTAMED BY
    COUNTLESS PAST BUDDHAS,
    THE BEINGS OF THIS DEGENERATE AGE, DIF-
    FICULT TO CURB;
    O COMPASSIONATE SAVIOR, I MAKE REQUESTS
    TO YOU.

This passage explains cultivating respect by reflecting upon
the kindness of the guru in the context of both the sutra and
tantra vehicles. It is a fact that up to now many buddhas have
come into the world system, and during the present precious
eon alone there have been previous buddhas, such as Ma-
hakasyapa; during their advents, however, we did not have the
opportunity to engage in the practice of dharma. Therefore,
we are more related to Shakyamuni Buddha. As explained in
the *De Lam Martid* (Practical Guide on the Stages of the Path),
your guru is kinder than all the buddhas and even kinder than
Buddha Shakyamuni. You should reflect: I, who have been
left behind by all the buddhas who appeared in the past, have
this opportunity to practice through your kindness alone. Contemplate what your fate would be if you were not under the
care of this guru. Thinking along such lines will enable you
to realize his great kindness.

47. AT THIS TIME OF SETTING OF THE SUN OF THE
    SAGE'S TEACHINGS,
    YOU ENACT THE DEEDS OF A CONQUEROR
    FOR THE MANY MIGRATORS WHO LACK A
    SAVIOR;
    O COMPASSIONATE SAVIOR, I MAKE REQUESTS
    TO YOU.

This passage speaks of how the root guru is kinder than Guru
Shakyamuni. Lord Buddha Shakyamuni appeared in India
more than twenty-five hundred years ago. He was such a great

being that even the mere sight of him or the least contact with him implanted a lot of virtuous imprints within the continuums of sentient beings. History records that he ripened the minds of many beings and placed them in the state of liberation. He engaged in such great activities, but during that time we were not able to have any personal relationship with him. If we had, our present situation would be different.

Similarly, we did not have the opportunity to meet the various great teachers such as the late masters of India, for example the seven successors of the Buddha, and Nagarjuna. In Tibet there were many masters during the initial dissemination of the dharma who fulfilled the wishes of many sentient beings, but we did not come under their care. And also during the later flourishing of the dharma there were many great masters of traditions like Sakya and Kadam; there were masters like Atisha and Ngok Legpai Sherab and Dromtompa and so forth. In the Kagyudpa sect there were great masters like Milarepa, Marpa and Gampopa. The doctrine of the Buddha became really very widespread in Tibet. Although such was the case, we did not have the karmic imprint to meet these teachers. Now we are in a very degenerate age; we can see conflict everywhere. You should contemplate that the guru's taking us into his care is indeed a very great kindness. To say it more plainly, if you had not been taken care of by this guru what would your fate have been? Think: It is only due to his kindness that I can be counted among human beings.

Through reflecting along these lines you will be able to see the great kindness of the guru. Make the request with mindfulness of that. Think in terms of, for example, being able to read because of the kindness of the person who first taught you the alphabet. Furthermore, because of the kindness of the person who taught you grammar and poetry and so forth, you are able to understand them. For the students of debate, right from the beginning, from the topic of colors,[29] you were taught by the guru. Because of that study, when you read the long and short versions of the lamrim, you do not have to leave the second part, the section on special insight, untouched, as do many people. You are at least able to have some level of understanding. That should help you to recollect the great kindness of the guru. For those who recite sadhanas such as that of Yamantaka, it is due to your teacher that you are able to follow it, right from the lineage prayers at the beginning. Then, when you attend teachings on the sadhana, you at least have some idea. It is not just because you attend my teachings, but rather because of the teacher who painstakingly and thoroughly taught you, that you get some idea. Although I am teaching you now, it is the teacher you live with daily and who guides you in a gradual process who is more kind. Then there are certain types of gurus who give us ordinations and vows and so forth; we can have the titles of novice and bikkshu and so forth because of the kindness of the guru who gave us these vows. In the same way, it is through the kindness of the vajra master that we can receive initiations and have the opportunity to practice them. You should reflect in such detail.

Also, most importantly, speaking of compassion and bodhicitta, which move our minds so much, the way we came into contact with such states of mind was through the guru. At the time of birth we were not familiar with such concepts at all. These points also apply to the understanding of emptiness. Developing even the mere interest in emptiness is the product of the guru's kindness, not to speak of having the chance to practice such guru yogas as *Lama Choepa*.

So, when you do this practice, from the point of view of qualifications there is no difference between Shakyamuni Buddha and your own root guru, but there is a great difference in terms of their kindness; thinking along these lines, you will be able to convince yourself of the value of your guru.

48. EVEN A SINGLE HAIR FROM THE PORES OF
    YOUR BODY
    IS PRAISED AS A FIELD OF MERIT FOR US
    HIGHER THAN THE CONQUERORS OF THE
    THREE TIMES AND TEN DIRECTIONS;
    O COMPASSIONATE SAVIOR, I MAKE REQUESTS
    TO YOU.

This passage is a reflection on the fact that the guru is the peerless field of merit as far as the individual practitioner is concerned. It has been explained in many tantras that making offerings to one's own root guru surpasses making offerings to infinite buddhas. You have this great opportunity to accumulate merit because you can see the guru with your naked eyes and listen to his speech, so you should make offerings, prostrations and so forth. Although such beings as Shakyamuni Buddha and Vajradhara and so on are very great, apart from on the imagination level there is no possibility for us to have contact with them in order to accumulate merit. Since through the guru we are also provided with the opportunity to make offerings to the infinite buddhas and bodhisattvas, we should see him as the highest field of merit. "Pores of your body" refers to the guru's attendants and also his pets which he holds very dear.

49. ADORNED BY THE PRECIOUS WHEELS AND THE THREE BODIES OF THOSE-GONE-TO-BLISS,
    FROM AN INTRICATE WEB OF APPEARANCES, WITH SKILLFUL MEANS
    YOU MANIFEST IN AN ORDINARY FORM TO LEAD ALL BEINGS;
    O COMPASSIONATE SAVIOR, I MAKE REQUESTS TO YOU.

This passage concerns making requests to the guru and expresses his qualities as a buddha's emanation body. In the commentary of Kachen Yeshe Gyaltsen, "inexhaustible chakras (wheels) of ornament" refers to the body, speech and mind of the guru. The body, speech and mind of the buddhas are like ornaments for sentient beings; they are inexhaustible in the sense that they are always engaged in the deeds of helping these beings. There are also specific meanings for "inexhaustible chakras of ornament" when explained individually in relation to the body, speech and mind of the guru. It says, "You are the manifestation of the body, speech and mind of all the buddhas which has assumed this ordinary appearance externally; and internally you are the manifestation of the inexhaustible chakras of ornament," which is also a reference to the body, speech and mind of the buddhas.

50. YOUR AGGREGATES, ELEMENTS, SENSORY
     BASES AND LIMBS
     ARE IN NATURE THE FIVE GONE-TO-BLISS,
     THEIR CONSORTS,
     BODHISATTVAS AND WRATHFUL PROTECTORS;
     O ESSENCE OF THE THREE JEWELS, SUPREME
     GURU, I MAKE REQUESTS TO YOU.

This passage speaks of the inner qualities of the guru, just as explained during the body mandala: that his aggregates and elements and so forth are actually in the nature of specific deities—"externally you assumed an ordinary form; internally, even the subtle parts of your body are the embodiment of the Three Jewels."

51. YOU ARE THE QUINTESSENCE OF TEN MIL-
     LION MANDALA CYCLES
     ARISING FROM THE PLAY OF OMNISCIENT PRIS-
     TINE AWARENESS,
     ALL-PERVADING LORD OF A HUNDRED
     BUDDHA FAMILIES, FOREMOST VAJ-
     RADHARA;
     O LORD OF PRIMORDIAL UNITY, I MAKE RE-
     QUESTS TO YOU.

This refers to the secret qualities, seeing the guru as the embodiment of the enjoyment body. "You arise as the enjoyment body from the manifestation of wisdom." This "ten million" mentioned here should not be understood literally, but rather should be taken to mean innumerable. Just as we find in the salutary verse of the lamrim text, "Homage to the Buddha, the Prince of the Sakya clan,/Whose body is born from a million virtues and good deeds,'' the Sanskrit term for ''million'' (*kunti*) has two meanings.

We also find similar lines in the text called *Lama Jangbod* (Calling the Guru From Afar):

> Whatever forms you assume, the hundred, five or three lineages
> [of isolated body], are all gurus;
> And the All-pervading Lord, the very source from which you sprang,
> Is also the guru himself.

This explains that the guru is the creator of all these buddha families and also that it is the guru into which all these elaborate buddha families dissolve—therefore he is called Pervading Lord. As he is the foremost lord of the families, he is called All-pervading Lord. ''Lord of Primordial Unity'' refers to the resultant state of union of the enjoyment body. Here one is making requesting prayers while seeing the guru as the enjoyment body and reflecting on his kindness.

52. UNOBSCURED, INSEPARABLE FROM THE PLAY OF SIMULTANEOUS BLISS,
   THE NATURE OF ALL THINGS, PERVADING EVERYTHING IN MOTION AND AT REST,
   SAMANTABHADRA, FREE OF BEGINNING OR END;
   ACTUAL ULTIMATE BODHICITTA, I MAKE REQUESTS TO YOU.

This stanza speaks of the guru's suchness qualities, from the point of view of seeing him as the truth body and reflecting upon his kindness. Explained in the context of the resultant state, ''unobscured'' refers to the state which is the manifestation of the spontaneous wisdom that is free of all obscurations. This refers to the ultimate wisdom which is inseparable from the objective emptiness. This explanation is according to the inseparability, or EVAM, of bliss and emptiness. Now to give the explanation according to the inseparable EVAM of the two truths: It says that the indivisibility of the wind and the mind is the basis of all the phenomena included within samsara and nirvana; it is all pervasive and is the source. Just as is said by Nagarjuna in his *Pancha-krama*, "One sees all the phenomena as alike in the sphere of meditative absorption on illusory nature."

Because it has retained its subtlety from beginningless time, this very subtle mind and wind is said to be without beginning and end. This is not a state of mind which sometimes becomes coarse and sometimes subtle due to changing circumstances as other mental states do, but rather it has retained its quality of subtlety right from beginningless time, and its nature is not penetrated by defilements. Just as explained in the *Uttaratantra*, all the defilements are adventitious. On the basis of this very subtle mind, all living beings have within themselves the inherent potential to achieve the unique qualities of buddhahood such as the ten powers.[30] Hence it is called the "all-good" in *Lama Choepa*. Conversely, the negative states of mind such as the afflictive emotions have the chance of arising actively as long as the gross levels of consciousness such as the eighty indicative conceptions are present. Once these are withdrawn, there is no chance for the arisal of negative states. So the meaning of the ultimate bodhicitta should be understood in terms of the union of the two truths; and the guru is the embodiment of such a union.

53. YOU ARE THE GURU, YOU ARE THE YIDAM, YOU ARE THE DAKINIS AND PROTECTORS; FROM NOW UNTIL ENLIGHTENMENT I SHALL SEEK NO REFUGE OTHER THAN YOU; IN THIS LIFE, THE BARDO AND ALL FUTURE LIVES HOLD ME WITH YOUR HOOK OF COMPASSION; SAVE ME FROM THE FEARS OF SAMSARA AND NIRVANA; GRANT ALL SIDDHIS;

BE MY CONSTANT FRIEND AND GUARD ME
FROM INTERFERENCES.

Here, we are requesting the guru with the special one-pointed
prayer, saying: You are the guru, so please release me from
the fears of samsara and nirvana (that is, the extreme of isolated peace); you are the meditational deity so grant me powerful attainments; you are the dakinis, so please be my compan-
ion; please help me on the path, and because you are the
dharmapala, please protect me from obstacles.

We are calling out to the guru saying: You are the guru, the
meditational deity etc., and apart from you I don't have any
refuge. We are entrusting ourselves entirely, saying: Come what
may, good or bad, I entrust myself entirely to you. This is
like driving in a stake without changing the position—the more
one hits it in the same spot the firmer it becomes. Hence the
analogy of driving in a stake—single-minded, cutting out any
second thoughts. Although there might be a special significance
to relating to various meditational deities, you should see all
the dharmapalas, dakinis and so forth as manifestations of your
own root guru. You should not have the notion that there is
a meditational deity separate from the guru, a dharmapala separate from the guru, or dakinis separate from the guru. If it
is convenient, you should do this prayer single-pointedly while
imagining touching the feet of the guru and entrusting yourself completely. Pray in this way three times.

54. BY THE VIRTUE OF HAVING THUS REQUESTED
    THREE TIMES,
    FROM THE SEATS OF MY GURU'S BODY, SPEECH
    AND MIND,
    WHITE, RED AND DARK BLUE NECTARS AND
    RAYS
    STREAM FORTH ONE BY ONE, AND THEN ALL
    TOGETHER, INTO MY OWN THREE PLACES.
    AND ONE BY ONE AND THEN ALL TOGETHER
    THEY ABSORB,

PURGING THE FOUR OBSCURATIONS, AND I RE-
CEIVE THE FOUR PURE EMPOWERMENTS
AND SEEDS OF THE FOUR BODIES; A DUPLI-
CATE OF THE GURU
HAPPILY DISSOLVES INTO ME AND GRANTS IN-
SPIRATION.

This is the taking of the four empowerments in the form of
a blessing. You can perform the receiving of initiations in a
more elaborate way. When doing this practice, focus your attention on the celestial mansion of the meditational deity that
you specialize in, and make requesting prayers. There are many
different versions, both elaborate and concise, for taking the
four initiations in connection with *Lama Choepa*. One version
is to first do the mandala offering, then make requesting
prayers, assume the two vows, generate the mind of all-
encompassing yoga and finally enter into the mandala. The
five wisdom initiations—water, crown, vajra, bell and name—
could be imagined being received individually or all together.
In the latter case, one invites the initiating deities all at once.
Next, do the vajra master initiation and so on. Then recite
the perfecting functions of the general vase initiation, of the
secret initiation, of the wisdom-knowledge initiation and of
the word initiation.

Next, imagine a duplicate of the Lama Lozang Thubwang
Dorje Chang dissolving into yourself; through the force of this
dissolution you melt into light from above and below, eventually dissolving into emptiness. This has to be done after having cultivated an understanding of union at the point of receiving the fourth initiation. When you are dissolved, from within
this clear light state you arise into a primordial being, the enjoyment body appropriate to your meditational deity. You can
imagine that you are actually arising into the illusory body and
visualize performing the practices of the mixings[31] of the waking state. Eventually, you return into the original body, thus
assuming the pride of being the emanation body.

If you wish to do an abbreviated form of this practice, imagine that you are blessed by the guru and dissolve into clear light. From within that clear light you arise into the primordial enjoyment body of the meditational deity in which you specialize.

After that, repeat the name mantras. At your heart and also at the heart of the central figure of the merit field, visualize the mantra circles: *om ah hum* in the middle; then the mantra circle *om ah vajradhara siddhi hum*, or *om vajradhara hum* (without *siddhi*). These are surrounded by *om mune mune maha munaye svaha*, or you can visualize *om mune mune maha mune shakyamuniye svaha*. Outside this is the name mantra of Lama Tsongkhapa: *om guru sumati kirti siddhi hum*. The name mantra of the root guru should be recited at this point, as well. It is also good to recite all the name mantras of the gurus from whom you have received teachings directly. If you know the name mantra in Sanskrit you should recite that; if not, just insert the name between *om guru vajradhara* and *hum*. It is not necessary to frantically search for the Sanskrit names. If you do this practice daily, it will keep you acquainted with the number of gurus you have and keep you constantly aware of their kindness. Otherwise, if someone were to ask offhand how many gurus you have, you would not be able to answer!

When you recite the praise verse of Lama Tsongkhapa, visualize a syllable MAM at the heart of Lama Lozang Thubwang Dorje Chang, and within the drop of the MAM visualize a blue HUM. Visualize the mantra circles at the heart of Lama Lozang Thubwang Dorje Chang.

When you are doing the repetition of mantra and the praise verse, it is very good to do what is called the "development of wisdom" visualization:

> Through the body vast wisdom; and the clear through
> speech;
> And through the scripture and sword and both,
> Shower the wisdoms of exposition, debate and composition.

If you can do that visualization it is very good. In order to practice it well, you should understand that just the altruistic attitude is not enough. It is necessary to increase your wisdom—this refers to the wisdom realizing emptiness—because the path on which we are embarking is the union of compassion and emptiness. Therefore, your practice of bodhicitta should be conjoined with the wisdom realizing emptiness. In order to increase this wisdom, make requesting prayers to Lama Lozang Thubwang Dorje Chang, and visualize nectars descending from his body. Retain your appearance as the deity, but relax the pride. When the nectars, which are in the nature of light rays, enter your body through the crown aperture, they purify all of your negativities and ignorance.

At this point, at the three parts of the body of Lama Tsongkhapa where you have visualized OM AH HUM, you could visualize Avalokiteshvara, Manjushri and, at the heart, Vajrapani. It is also mentioned that one could visualize the inner, outer and secret aspects of Avalokiteshvara at the crown, of Manjushri at the throat and of Vajrapani at the heart—this is like a nine-being deity. There are many different aspects of Manjushri, and a visualization of a nine-being Manjushri has been explained in the *Kachem Lung Kurma* commentary. Nectars, their atoms in the aspect of Manjushris, flow from the bodies of the Manjushris, filling your body and purifying your defilements and eliminating your ignorance. Light rays, radiating in all directions, make offerings to the buddhas and bodhisattvas, and draw forth all their blessings, especially vast intelligence, in the aspect of Manjushris of various sizes which enter you; imagine your intelligence becoming equal to that of Manjushri. Through speech you gain clear intelligence, and through the seed syllable DHI—the seed syllable of Manjushri—swift intelligence.

Vast intelligence, or wisdom, refers to the intelligence of a wide perspective which encompasses a wide range of topics; clear intelligence refers to the wisdom which discriminates even the most subtle differences; swift intelligence refers to the wisdom which can perform these feats within the shortest possible time. Profound intelligence, obtained through visualization of the hand symbols, refers to the type of wisdom that is never confused by even the most difficult themes and can explore the scriptures in both their explicit and implicit meanings. Wisdom with such qualities is like that of great scholars such as Gungtang Rinpoche.

Here the nine-round visualization for increasing wisdom is explained. These nine are: the vast, clear, swift, and profound; composition, debating and teaching; and then the two visualizations explained earlier—those of cleansing the negativities and eliminating ignorance.

There are also many different techniques explained for engaging in peaceful activities, such as those for overcoming illnesses, based on this practice. Activities of increase, influence and ferocity can be undertaken as well. If you are doing a practice for the prolongation of life, at the heart of Lama Lozang Thubwang Dorje Chang you can visualize a deity such as White Tara or Amitayus, at whose heart are the mantra circles. You can also generate yourself into that particular deity, instantly changing appearance and divine pride. Then, by focusing on the mantra circle, you can do the visualization for the prolongation of life. You can also do it without visualizing Amitayus at the heart of Lama Lozang Thubwang Dorje Chang, but rather, by focusing your attention on the Amitayus who is in the merit field and then doing the visualization. Similarly, you can perform the activities of increasing wealth by visualizing Vaisravana and other deities of wealth. So, all these types of activities could be undertaken on the basis of this practice of "Migtsema," the praise verses of Lama Tsongkhapa.

When you visualize Avalokiteshvara, Manjushri and Vajrapani at the respective parts of the body of Lama Tsongkhapa, he should be seen as the embodiment of these three deities. You can also engage in the various visualizations for the dual purposes of helping sentient beings and of making offerings to the buddhas. Do the recitation of the name mantras of all the gurus. After that you can recite a verse of dedication such as:

By this virtuous action
May I attain the state of the gurus and their children

And lead all beings without exception
To that same state as well.

A slightly shorter version of receiving the four initiations is as follows. Nectars descend from the body of Lama Lozang Thubwang Dorje Chang and you receive the vase initiation; Vajradhara enters into union with the consort, the bodhicittas melt and you receive the secret initiation; their realization of emptiness and experience of great bliss constitutes the wisdom-knowledge initiation; by reflecting upon the meaning of union you receive the word initiation.

The shortest version is as found in the manual here. White, red and blue light rays and nectars emerge sequentially from the three syllables at the three parts of the guru's body and enter into your own body, purifying the related negativities, and you receive the first three initiations accordingly. At the point where the three light rays dissolve into you collectively, you receive the fourth initiation. At that point it is important to reflect on the meaning of union. After that, a duplicate of the guru dissolves into you with great joy.

If you do this visualization without taking the bodhisattva and tantric vows it is like a blessing, but if you do the most elaborate version, taking the two vows and so forth, that actually serves as a self-initiation practice. Therefore, it can restore broken vows and commitments, providing you have done the necessary approximation of the deity, the retreat. I do not know whether this will serve for giving initiation to others, but for one's own practice this will serve as a self-initiation.

6 Reviewing the Entire Stages of the Path

In the following practice, you receive blessings by reviewing the entire path of sutra and tantra. Visualize all sentient beings around you. If you are alone and have the leisure, reflect on the practice of guru devotion and think from the depth of your heart: There is no refuge superior to my own root guru. With such reinforcement of conviction, you should reflect on the fact that all the buddhas of the ten directions have assumed this ordinary form as your root guru in order to tame you. With such understanding, cultivate strong faith and also respect. Request the guru to take care of you, not only in this lifetime but throughout all future lives. Then do the recitation from here onwards. When you make this request, imagine that the guru consents to it and is pleased by the determination you have made. Nectars descend from the body of the guru, enter your body and the bodies of all sentient beings, and all the negativities, especially those committed in connection with guru devotion practice, are purified just as in the refuge practice. Think that all the sentient beings and yourself have the strong faith capable of seeing the guru as a true buddha and the respect required for realization of guru devotion.

The subsequent explanation will be according to the outlines of *Jhangchub Lamrim Chenmo* by Lama Tsongkhapa.

84. O HOLY AND VENERABLE GURUS, SUPREME
    FIELD OF MERIT,
    INSPIRE ME TO MAKE OFFERINGS AND
    DEVOTED REQUESTS
    TO YOU, O PROTECTORS AND ROOT OF ALL
    WELL-BEING,
    THAT I MAY COME UNDER YOUR JOYOUS CARE.

This verse deals with the first outline, which explains the proper modes of reliance on the guru, the foundation of all the paths.

85. INSPIRE ME TO REALIZE HOW THIS OPPOR-
    TUNE AND FORTUNATE REBIRTH
    IS RARE AND FOUND BUT ONCE AND QUICKLY
    LOST,
    AND THEREBY, UNDISTRACTED BY THE
    MEANINGLESS WORKS OF THIS LIFE,
    TO SEIZE ITS MEANINGFUL ESSENCE.

The second outline, the stages of training the mind on the basis of such a reliance, begins with this passage, which in turn is divided into two. The first part attempts to induce the practitioner to take the essence of the precious human form, by explaining the rarity and great value of it. The verse explains how this form is endowed with leisures and opportunities. We have now in our hands this once-obtained opportunity of having a fully endowed human existence which generally is something almost impossible to achieve. Having identified the endowments and the value of such an opportunity, decide: I must engage in the practice of dharma, for if I were to return from such an opportunity empty-handed it would be a great loss.

The actual practice of taking the essence of the human form is divided into three sections, in the context of the three scopes—the small scope, the middling scope and the highest scope. Topics such as impermanence are meditated on. "Rare and found but once and quickly lost" or "realizing the nature of swift disintegration" explains impermanence. Since we are produced phenomena, we are subject to change and all of us have to die. Since a produced phenomenon is caused by a condition, it is impermanent; the mere fact of being produced is cause enough for a phenomenon's disintegration, because disintegration does not require a second cause. The potential for disintegration is inherent in mere production. Generally speaking, the word *production* has a positive sense, and *impermanence* has a more negative connotation, implying disintegration. Superficially, they sound opposing; but when we probe deeper we find that production itself is in the nature of destruction. This does not apply to external phenomena alone; in thinking about it, you should focus rather upon your own aggregates. We are born due to neither the blessings of the Buddha nor some neutral force, but rather through the force of the actions we committed in the past. Being impermanent, we are dependent on other factors. Dharmakirti's statement, "In the nature of suffering because of being impermanent"[32] is really very powerful. We are products of our own actions, therefore we are subject to suffering. Being by nature impermanent shows we are dependent upon causes and conditions, and in this case *causes and conditions* refers to our karmic actions and the defilements. As long as we let ourselves be under the influence of the negative states of mind, there is no place for happiness. For example, as long as we Tibetans are under the tyranny of the Chinese communists, there is no chance of happiness. We have no independence; we are other-powered and dependent upon other factors. In our case, we also are other-powered in that we are under the influence or power of negative actions and emotional afflictions, which in turn have their root in the self-grasping attitude, the notion of the inherent existence of phenomena, which is a distorted consciousness.

You should contemplate along these lines upon the coarse

levels of impermanence and also the subtle levels. Take, for example, ourselves: Although we have taken a birth, we are already in the process of aging and approaching death. Ours is a birth with a complete potential for aging and death. It is only your practice of dharma that will help at the time of death. The continuity of this consciousness will go on, although the present body will be left behind. All the phenomena on which this physical form depends, like wealth, shelter, strength and so forth, will not help and will not go with you to your future lifetime. It is only the continuity of the consciousness which will accompany you. If you gather any virtuous qualities on the basis of this consciousness, you will be able to carry them along. I think I can say that even when we talk about mental qualities based on the gross level of mind, the more familiarity with them we cultivate the more we can leave imprints upon the subtle consciousness. For example, when one has a very strong force of mind upon a given object during the waking time, during sleep one can experience it with a subtle consciousness in dreams. This shows that the two levels of mind are complementary to each other. So, the more familiarity we have even at the coarser levels of consciousness, the stronger the impression on the subtle levels will be. If you have a very strong wish to get up early you can wake up at that time, although during the sleeping state the consciousness was subtle. In the same way, if you wish to bring about some effect in the future life through your practice of dharma, you should not adopt a relaxed style of practice but rather should be very forceful and practice with awareness. I think that the deeper the level of one's practice, the more transformation it can bring about and the more it can affect one. So, it is only the practice of dharma that helps at such times.

Here the meditations upon the rarity of the precious human form and impermanence are mentioned together. Being mindful of its nature of momentary disintegration, you should not waste even the shortest moment of the human life. Having recited this stanza, imagine nectars descending from the body of the central figure and entering into you, and yourself attaining the realization of the rarity of the precious human form and its impermanence.

I. THE STAGES COMMON TO SMALL SCOPE

86. AFRAID AS I AM OF THE SEARING BLAZE OF
    SUFFERING IN THE LOWER REALMS,
    INSPIRE ME TO TAKE HEARTFELT REFUGE IN
    THE THREE PRECIOUS GEMS
    AND TO FERVENTLY STRIVE AT AVOIDING NON-
    VIRTUE AND
    ACCOMPLISHING ALL COLLECTIONS OF
    VIRTUE.

Reflect upon the sufferings of the lower realms: the hell, animal and hungry ghost realms. Regarding the hell realms, it is quite difficult to accept what is written in abhidharma and related texts, but irrespective of whether there are such hell realms or not, we can infer that there is a state with the utmost suffering. I often say, for example, that since we have this physical body with brain cells and so forth, we do not have any doubt about its existence; but if we were to explain the structure of a body with its nervous system, and especially the brain cells, to a person from a different planet, he would have a hard time believing it. It would be difficult to convince him. In the same way, if we are shown various types of insects and plants through a magnifying glass, we become convinced of their existence, but if somebody were to tell us that there are these insects and so forth when we had not seen them, it would be difficult to believe that there is such diversity of life. So, because we have not experienced the hells during this lifetime, it is not easy for us to be convinced. We tend to think, "Is there such a thing?" Yet it is also difficult to prove that they do not exist. The best we can do is say, "I hope that such realms don't exist at all!"

The nature of karma, or action, is very complex and inconceivable. We know that taming and improving one's mind bring about happiness even within this lifetime. From this we can infer that through training of the mind one can also cultivate high realizations which ultimately lead to the omniscient state. Factors which train the mind toward such a noble aim are the positive aspects of the mind. Regarding the opposite, if you think about it, you will find that gross emotional afflictions like anger and so forth cause a lot of unhappiness. This almost leads us to infer that such unfortunate and suffering realms do exist. If one believes that through the force of virtuous actions one can achieve a better form and live in a better place and so forth, one can likewise infer that one's negative actions actually bring undesirable consequences such as rebirth in lower realms.

We know that there are two types of rebirth caused by tamed and untamed states of mind respectively. Although the human form is a product of a good state of mind, still we suffer in obvious ways starting right from the time of birth. So, we can see that the human form is actually a product of more or less equal proportions of actions based on good and bad states of mind. When the better states of mind are more forceful, the result is purer and higher, such as rebirth in the higher realms, as gods of the desire realm, form realm and formless realm. As these rebirths are still in cyclic existence, they have their root in the ignorant mind of the self-grasping attitude. Due to different degrees of force of the virtuous states of mind, the results are of a different nature. In the same way, the more forceful the negative states of mind are, the more suffering effects they will bring. Whether one takes rebirth in a higher state or not is determined by the state of mind that one has now. So, if one is different from an ordinary person because of having virtuous attitudes, then one has hope of experiencing a higher state in the future. That is the meaning of saying that your future fate is in your own hands. So, we are presently at a crossroads.

In the lower realm of the animals, pets are slightly better off, but, for example, the fish in the ocean have to experience a situation where the large ones eat the smaller ones. They have to spend their life in such a state, and there is no possibility for them to accumulate virtue. There is some chance for animals on the surface of the earth to accumulate virtues. A verse says:

> If someone looks at a figure of Buddha in a mural,
> even when his mental state is disturbed,
> He will still accumulate merits to have the vision
> of millions of buddhas in the future.

Those in the ocean are afflicted by the actions of human beings too. Far from holding them dear, the attitude of others towards them is not as sentient beings but rather as food. It is really pitiable. These creatures have a life which they definitely hold most dear, just as we do; they have the self-cherishing attitude too. The only consolation is that once they get caught and brought onto dry ground they do not have long to suffer. These suffering states are obvious and visible to us. When one thinks along these lines, it is actually quite frightening to eat meat. In a place where one has all the necessary conditions—vegetables and so forth—it is best to be vegetarian. But if you have to consider your health and take into account the environment, then it is a different matter. So, the suffering of animals on just this planet is something infinite.

Having reflected upon the state of the animals, think that whether you will be reborn into such a state or not will be determined by your own karma. Having contemplated upon such fearful states, one should take refuge, which is the gateway to becoming a buddhist. The most important thing is to reflect on the qualities of the dharma. Here it is very important to have some understanding of the structures of the reasonings outlined in the texts on logic which prove the existence of a state of cessation. Inference of the existence of this state can be developed by realizing the fact that our mental defilements are adventitious and therefore can be separated from the essential nature of the mind. Such a realization, however, depends upon the understanding of emptiness according to the madhyamaka prasangika school of thought and its unique view of the nature of mental defilements. Generally, when we have a gross experience of desire, hatred, etc., we find that our apprehension as inherently existing of the object upon which we have such strong forces of emotion is also very forceful. Although during both neutral and strongly emotional states the appearance of inherent nature is always present, during the latter it is more forceful and obvious. Therefore, you can identify the object of negation on the basis of such experiences. When you have a very strong force of attachment, you feel the object of your emotion is independent, the most supreme, not subject to change, as though it were permanently good. This process also applies to other negative states of mind like hatred: You find the object of hatred to be truly the worst person, the most repulsive, etc. Of the two states—having a stronger force of emotion and not—we know definitely that the latter is more comfortable.

Although negative states of mind like hatred and the self-grasping attitude are very forceful, they do not have a valid support, or a sound foundation. On the other hand, an understanding of emptiness, although it might be very weak at the initial stage, has a valid foundation, and therefore has the potential to be increased to the utmost level. Consequently, the more we search for and analyze emptiness, the clearer and more valid it becomes, whereas when we examine the process of apprehension of the negative states of mind, the less valid they appear and eventually they are seen to be totally distorted. Such states as the understanding of emptiness are virtuous qualities based on the consciousness. Unlike the heat of water or the athletic prowess of a sportsman—which are physical qualities and are hence unstable—these mental abilities have a very firm and stable basis. Because they are virtuous qualities based on the mind, they have the potential to be increased to the utmost level without having to depend on a renewed effort once one has gained familiarity with them. So, there really is something called the dharma.

At the moment it might be difficult to infer the existence

146 *The Union of Bliss and Emptiness*

of something like the truth of cessation. Although it is difficult for me to explain out of my own experience, I think one can understand that defilements have the potential to be purified. If such a thing called cessation does not exist, it is one matter; but if such a thing does exist, there is indeed a great hope. Such a state is actually the true release from bondage. When you reflect on dharma, think that the Buddha himself experienced this state and has shown the path leading to it; therefore he is non-deceiving. The companions that one seeks, the sangha community, are the ones following a true teacher and traveling on the right path. Thus you will find the meaning of the Three Jewels quite profound. As explained in *Jhangchub Lamrim Chenmo*, one cannot just spontaneously attain the experience of the resultant dharma of cessation by remaining idle and enjoying leisure; it has to be brought about through constant meditation and practice.

In order to realize such a state of cessation, you first have to restrain yourself from indulging in negativities. Therefore, it is necessary to refrain from the ten non-virtuous actions.[33] In the text, the reasons for refraining from these ill deeds are explained, with an explication of the law of cause and effect coming at this point. This is well founded, because the law of cause and effect dictates that if one does good one will experience comfort, and if one does evil one will experience suffering. This law is not made by a creator or buddha, but is a natural law. In order to experience happiness one has to refrain from negative actions. As it says in Vasubhandu's *Abhidharmakosha*:

> When condensed, the virtuous and non-virtuous actions
> are contained within the ten actions.

The restraints which are adopted through proper application of the antidotes are called the ten virtuous actions.

Observing the law of cause and effect is the precept of refuge. One who is practicing *Lama Choepa* has to base his practice on what is written here. One does not make the distinction between good or bad practitioners of *Lama Choepa* on the basis of their clarity of visualization alone. Those who claim to be practitioners of *Lama Choepa* and do not follow the law of cause and effect are not proper practitioners; they are just like drawings of practitioners. If one denies the existence of the law of cause and effect, one is acting against the advice of the spiritual guru, since the gurus advise us to follow the law of karma. Such a denial also constitutes contradicting the precepts in relation to the Three Jewels. It is you yourself who will be the loser, for there is no difference on the part of the Three Jewels. Following the law of cause and effect should be taken not as something which helps the dharma, but rather, as an act which helps your own happiness. You should not have the notion: Although I do not need the dharma personally, if I do not practice, the Buddha's doctrine might degenerate. This is the wrong type of attitude. Kentsang Jamyang Rinpoche said in his *Chagchen Zindri* (Notes on Mahamudra), a meditation manual on emptiness: "If one has the notion that one's practice of dharma contributes towards the dharma, or does a favor for the dharma, that is a wrong attitude."

II. THE STAGES COMMON TO MIDDLING SCOPE

87. VIOLENTLY TOSSED AS I AM BY WAVES OF DE-
    LUSIONS AND KARMA,
    PLAGUED BY HORDES OF SEA-MONSTERS—THE
    THREE SUFFERINGS—
    INSPIRE ME TO DEVELOP AN INTENSE LONG-
    ING TO BE FREE
    OF THIS DREADFUL BOUNDLESS GREAT
    OCEAN OF EXISTENCE.

This passage outlines a reflection on the general sufferings of samsara and on the nature of the truths of suffering and its origins, which enables us to understand the process by which we rotate in this cyclic existence. It talks of the four noble truths. When the Buddha taught dharma, he first taught the four noble truths. This topic is very vast. Although one has to meditate on the rarity of the precious human form and so forth, I think reflecting on these truths brings about more change within one's mental continuum. If at the beginning one cannot identify the dharma and develop the certainty that it has great value, then one will not be able to engage in proper practice. Sometimes I feel the sequence of the lamrim should be more modelled on the sequence of the four noble truths as explained by the Buddha himself. In the lamrim are described the sufferings of the hell realms, but it is quite difficult to convince people of their existence and for them to imagine them. Doing so is actually not necessary, because we have enough sufferings with our own body on this planet, so one can just reflect on those. We have taken rebirths for innumerable lifetimes and the continuity of the consciousness goes on. Even if you think you will go on taking rebirth as a human being, you can reflect on the sufferings of the human beings: firstly of birth, then of growing up, becoming old and dying again, and so forth. If you were to continue in this cycle, let us say hundreds, thousands and millions of times, there is really not much sense in it. Therefore, if there is any possibility of putting an end to this meaningless rotation, it is high time we searched for it.

Our "leader" is actually the defilements and negative actions. If one is not able to revolt against and overcome those, the most harmful factors, then one is not really a human being. If instead one preserves them within oneself and always puts the blame on external harmful spirits and thinks of them as one's worst enemies, this is actually quite contradictory to the practice of bodhicitta. If I were a harmful spirit and someone pointed his finger at me and said, "You are a harmful spirit," I would be happy because that shows that my accuser has not been able to identify his own enemy, and hence is vulnerable to my harms. If one actually practices bodhicitta properly and views all beings as friends, then harmful spirits will not harm one, for one will be invulnerable.

The emotional afflictions such as attachment are termed the

"arrows of flowers," because, like flower arrows, they cannot pierce anything violently, yet they influence us in a kind of gentle way. Defilements are very harmful. When we have them in an obvious and manifest way we forget about their destructive nature. If, under the influence of these harmful factors you indulge in negative actions, it is definite that you will have to experience the consequences. So, being sick, for example, is actually the consequence of your own past actions. It is possible that there might be slight harm from others such as external spirits, but mainly it is the consequence of your own actions. In the same way, the happiness that you experience is basically the consequence of your own actions; the dharmapalas might provide circumstantial assistance that could lead to an earlier fruition of the actions, and then take the whole credit for it! As a result they are rewarded with torma offerings!

When anger arises, reactions like shouting at people and insulting them and so forth naturally follow; it is very spontaneous, and you will indulge in negative actions. Uncomfortable consequences are actually experienced right at that moment. At that instant even your facial expression changes and you feel very uncomfortable and uptight; that is just the beginning of the suffering. As a result, when one indulges in a negative action it leaves an imprint on the consciousness. When we talk of the base on which the imprints on the consciousness are left, it is of two types: the enduring base which is the mere I, and the temporary base which is the consciousness. These lines of a prayer written by the First Dalai Lama Gedun Drubpa help a lot:

Reflect upon the kindness of all beings in general,
And cultivate respect towards spiritual persons in particular.

So long as the defilements are not extinguished, one can never overcome suffering completely; therefore, until such a stage is attained, suffering remains infinite. I think that among the practitioners of lamrim there are those who have strong faith in the dharma. For those who have strong faith but do not have much understanding, it is good to be guided beginning with the contemplation on the rarity of the precious human form. But, as suggested earlier, there are certain types of people whom it is better to guide on the basis of the four noble truths, even though, seen from a superficial view, it may seem that they are being led on the middling scope before the small scope. Such guidance will give them a very comprehensive understanding, because when someone is guided according to that sequence it is natural that he or she will see the potential of the precious human form and its value. One can see that the guru is very valuable though such a process. Otherwise, if the value of the guru is established by citing quotations from the sutras and tantras right at the beginning, it will be difficult to accept for a certain kind of person. First of all he or she will question the validity of the scripture itself.

88. I HAVE ABANDONED THE VIEW THAT SEES
    THIS UNBEARABLE PRISON
    OF CYCLIC EXISTENCE AS A PLEASURE GROVE;
    INSPIRE ME TO MAINTAIN THE THREE TRAIN-
    INGS, THE STORE OF THE ARYAS' TREASURES,
    AND THEREBY HOLD THE BANNER OF
    LIBERATION.

What is meant by "cyclic existence" in this passage is the state where emotional afflictions are given the upper hand and kept unharmed. No matter what kind of prosperous lives you may enjoy as a human being or deva, you will still be found in cyclic existence. You might even achieve a higher state of birth like the "peak of existence," at which stage you temporarily do not experience sufferings or even gross, fluctuating happiness, remaining only in a very neutral state. In this state, the gross conceptual thoughts have ceased, so you temporarily experience great peace and bliss, something akin to an absorption into a state of cessation, for a long time. But since you will still have the self-grasping attitude within you, you will not have achieved liberation. As long as there are defilements within you, there will be no happiness. Therefore, cyclic existence is compared to a prison. The reference to holding "the banner of liberation" is to the practice of morality, more in the context of the middling scope. The training in calm abiding and special insight are explained in *Lama Choepa* in the section on great scope.

III. THE STAGES OF GREAT SCOPE

89. I HAVE CONSIDERED HOW ALL THESE TORMENTED BEINGS ARE
MY MOTHERS WHO HAVE KINDLY CARED FOR ME AGAIN AND AGAIN;
INSPIRE ME TO DEVELOP UNFEIGNED COMPASSION
LIKE THAT OF A LOVING MOTHER FOR HER PRECIOUS CHILD.

This passage outlines the practice of bodhicitta. In *Kachem Lung Kurma*, Yongdzin Yeshe Gyaltsen is quoted:

The bodhisattvas of higher faculties train according to the techniques of exchanging oneself for others,
And bodhisattvas of lower faculties train according to the techniques of the seven-point cause and effect method.

In both cases you cultivate loving-kindness. In order to achieve genuine bodhicitta, it is necessary to have compassion, which in turn depends upon having developed loving-kindness focused upon all beings. Regarding the techniques for cultivating such compassion, two major systems have emerged: the seven-point cause and effect method and the method of equalizing and exchanging oneself with others. In this text both of these systems are integrated into a single method.

Having recognized others as mothers and having recollected their kindness, one has to repay them. The more forceful your loving-kindness, the more forceful will be your generation of compassion and love and also the unusual attitude.

90. AS NO-ONE DESIRES EVEN THE SLIGHTEST
    SUFFERING
    NOR EVER HAS ENOUGH OF HAPPINESS,
    THERE IS NO DIFFERENCE BETWEEN MYSELF
    AND OTHERS;
    THEREFORE, INSPIRE ME TO REJOICE WHEN
    OTHERS ARE HAPPY.

This passage explains the practice of exchanging oneself with others. For this practice there are no techniques superior to those outlined in the *Bodhisattvacharyavatara* with which you are probably quite familiar. In addition to the self-grasping attitude, the self-cherishing attitude is viewed by the bodhisattvas as one of their arch-enemies. For us, these two types of consciousness, the self-cherishing attitude and the self-grasping attitude, are like twins. They reside within us as inseparable; they assist each other. Through the force of gaining the direct realization of emptiness and the path of meditation, you can abandon the self-grasping attitude. So, at that stage the self-cherishing attitude alone remains. This self-cherishing attitude has many different levels, subtle and coarser. For a very powerful bodhisattva who has not yet abandoned the delusions, the self-cherishing attitude would not be as forceful as the self-grasping attitude. But the self-grasping and self-cherishing attitudes within us stay at leisure, because we do not revolt against them. We read the root text on wisdom, we recite the *Lama Choepa*, but it does not affect them at all. Nothing poses any threat to them.

From here onwards, the text explains the disadvantages of the self-cherishing attitude and the advantages of the attitude which cherishes the welfare of others.

91. THIS CHRONIC DISEASE OF CHERISHING
    MYSELF
    IS THE CAUSE OF UNWANTED SUFFERING;
    PERCEIVING THIS, MAY I BE INSPIRED TO
    BLAME, BEGRUDGE

AND DESTROY THIS MONSTROUS DEMON OF
SELF-CHERISHING.

92. CHERISHING MY MOTHERS AND SEEKING TO
SECURE THEM IN BLISS
IS THE GATEWAY TO INFINITE VIRTUES;
SEEING THIS, MAY I BE INSPIRED TO HOLD
THEM DEARER THAN MY LIFE,
EVEN SHOULD THEY ARISE AS MY ENEMIES.

93. IN BRIEF, INFANTILE BEINGS LABOR FOR
THEIR OWN GAIN ONLY,
WHILE THE BUDDHAS WORK SOLELY FOR
OTHERS;
UNDERSTANDING THE DISTINCTIONS BE-
TWEEN THEIR RESPECTIVE FAULTS AND
VIRTUES,
MAY I BE INSPIRED TO BE ABLE TO EXCHANGE
MYSELF FOR OTHERS.

These passages explain the possibility of exchanging oneself
with others. It says here in the root text that it is not necessary to explain the practice elaborately, but in short one can
see the disadvantages and advantages of cherishing oneself and
others merely by comparing oneself and the Buddha.

Meditation on Equanimity
Kyabje Trijang Rinpoche had a very unique meditation on the
cultivation of equanimity, explaining it in the context of the
conventional and ultimate truths.

1. The first section, that dealing with conventional truth, is
divided into two points: a) the viewpoint of others, and b) the
viewpoint of oneself. These in turn are each divided into three:

a) the three factors for cultivating equanimity from the viewpoint of others are described below.
    The first is the thought that all sentient beings, including

yourself, do not desire suffering and therefore there is no point in being partial or discriminatory.

The second is the recognition that sentient beings and oneself equally desire happiness, yet lack it; therefore, there is no point in discriminating. It is like a situation when there are many beggars—there is no reason to make any discrimination between them when we give to them.

The first point is the summary and the second one is the elaboration.

The third explains that all sentient beings are equal in lacking happiness. Although they desire happiness and shun suffering, they are afflicted by suffering. Analogously, if a lot of patients are afflicted by the same illness, there is no reason for discriminating between them when treating them.

These are the three factors from the viewpoint of others. One trains in the attitude, "I shall never discriminate between beings when I help them overcome sufferings and gain happiness."

b) The three factors for cultivating equanimity from the viewpoint of oneself have to do with the idea that if one wants to look at things from the viewpoint of others, it is necessary that one should see them all as equal to oneself.

Firstly, one might have the thought, "Among others, some harm me and some help me," and thus might try to justify having a discriminatory attitude. Then one should reflect upon the fact that all sentient beings have been one's relatives and mothers, friends and so forth. They have helped one in the past and they are helping one now, and they will also help one in the future. Through such lines of reasoning, one reaches the conclusion that there is no justification for discrimination.

Secondly, one might then have the thought, "Although beings may occasionally help me, still they remain either harmful or neutral, and the neutral persons can be neglected because they are actually unrelated to me at all." Such an attitude is also wrong. To give an example: Although all the persons who contributed to the building of this temple, such as those who sold the rods and the cement and so forth, are not here, indirectly they have been helpful to us. So, when one thinks along these lines, one finds that there are more occasions when others help and fewer occasions when they harm. Enemies are especially very kind, because they serve as an impetus for one's own practice, as is explained thoroughly in the *Bodhisattvacharyavatara*. That is the second technique for cultivating equanimity.

Thirdly, one might realize that for one's part one is under the influence of karma and many defilements and likewise the other sentient beings are under the influence of karma and defilements. As explained in the *Bodhisattvacharyavatara*, there is no point in one who is in the nature of impermanence, suffering and conventionality having hatred towards someone who has the same nature.

2. The second section explains the cultivation of equanimity in the ultimate sense. (This "ultimate" should not be taken to refer to the ultimate truth of emptiness—rather, it means that the explanation is relatively ultimate in comparison to the sense of the preceding section).

Firstly, if there is such a phenomenon as a person who is a permanent enemy who has to be eliminated, then the Buddha, who has an omniscient mind, should see him. Buddha has not seen such a person; he saw all people as friends. Also, the enemies and friends are actually relatives. Just as Gungtang Rinpoche said:

Even your best friend of today,
If caught up in a slight misunderstanding caused by a few
 unsettling words,
Could turn into your worst enemy tomorrow;
So, the question of near and distant ends there.

Secondly, these "enemies" are changeable, so they are not permanent. Just as is explained in Aryadeva's *Chatu-Shataka Shastra*, "If there is an ultimate enemy, the Buddha should see him; and such a person should not change, which is not the case."

Thirdly, as explained in *The Compendium of Deeds*, enemy and friend are actually posited in dependence upon each other and are therefore only relative. We can say that enemies and friends do exist on a conventional or relative level, but what we are actually trying to prevent is the negative states of mind of hatred and attachment associated with enemy and friend. We are not stopping the recognition of someone as enemy and friend, but are trying to prevent our fluctuating emotions based on there being enemies and friends at a relative level. For example, the Buddha sees all the sentient beings as friends, but he does not generate any attachment. There actually are harmful spirits who impede the flourishing of the dharma, but one should not have hatred towards them just because of that. The lines of reasoning in this third point do not actually negate the conventional existence of the enemy and friend, but rather they negate the inherent existence of enemy and friend. It is this apprehension of enemy and friend as inherently existent which gives rise to the negative states of mind such as hatred and attachment.

So, altogether nine points of meditation for cultivating equanimity have been explained. They are very profound. These methods are arranged and explained in a very practical way and have their source in the *Bodhisattvacharyavatara* and also *Ratnavali*. It is very good to study and practice these two texts in conjunction.

If you are going to practice the two major techniques for cultivating bodhicitta in an integrated way, first you should cultivate equanimity. This is the equanimity which is also common the lower vehicles; hence equanimity is likened to a smooth ground which is moistened by love, as described by a master in the following verse:

I invoke your inspiration, O Omniscient One—
You have attained the supreme fruit of the bodhicitta tree,
Born from the seed of unceasing compassion,
Moistened by love in the soil of equanimity.

The order of generation is: 1) equanimity; 2) recognition

of all beings as mothers; 3) recollection of their kindness; 4) repaying their kindness; at that point, 5) special equanimity which is cultivated from the viewpoint of oneself and others; 6) reflection on the disadvantages of the self-cherishing attitude; 7) understanding the advantages of cherishing others. From this arises a very unique loving-kindness which is induced by the attitude of exchanging oneself for others. It is quite different from the love generated earlier. This state of loving-kindness is much more forceful than the one cultivated and induced by recognizing the mothers, recollecting their kindness and repaying it. Then comes the actual exchange of oneself with others. This is in turn followed by the practice of 8) giving and 9) taking, which are induced by love and compassion respectively; and then 10) development of the special unusual attitude, which leads on to 11) the cultivation of actual bodhicitta.

94. CHERISHING MYSELF IS THE DOORWAY TO ALL
    DOWNFALLS,
    WHILE CHERISHING MY MOTHERS IS THE
    FOUNDATION OF EVERYTHING GOOD;
    INSPIRE ME TO MAKE THE CORE OF MY
    PRACTICE
    THE YOGA OF EXCHANGING MYSELF FOR
    OTHERS.

Here you must develop the conviction, "There is no practice superior to the practice of exchanging oneself for others. This is the essence of all the teachings; hence I shall devote all my effort to engaing in this great practice of 'giving and taking'."

95. THEREFORE, O VENERABLE COMPASSIONATE
    GURUS,
    BLESS ME THAT ALL KARMIC OBSCURATIONS
    AND SUFFERINGS
    OF MOTHER MIGRATORS RIPEN UPON ME
    RIGHT NOW,

AND THAT I MAY GIVE OTHERS MY HAPPINESS
AND VIRTUOUS DEEDS
IN ORDER THAT ALL SENTIENT BEINGS HAVE
HAPPINESS.

This is the actual practice, done in connection with the visualization of giving and taking. It was explained by Nagarjuna in *Ratnavali* thus:

> May their negative fruits ripen upon me,
> And my positive fruits upon them.

When Panchen Lama Lozang Choekyi Gyaltsen first composed this text, the first line was not included. Because it is very powerful, he was requested to insert one more line. Therefore, there are five lines in this verse. Having reflected on the advantages and disadvantages of the two types of attitudes, at the point when one has actually brought about a certain change within one's mental continuum, one calls out to the guru, "Hence I request, O most compassionate guru, may the negative obscurations and sufferings of all other sentient beings instantly come upon me and may I be able to share my virtues and happiness with other sentient beings." It is good to recite this verse three times at least.

Although in the text we find the sufferings, obscurations and negativities mentioned together, when you do the practice you should rather visualize them individually, as you recite them. First, all the sufferings in the form of a black heap, or cloud, or in the form of black liquids dissolve into the depth of your heart at the point where you usually visualize the concentration being. It is the spot where you have the strong feeling of "I." Imagine them dissolving into your indestructible drop. During the second repetition, all the causes of these sufferings—the self-grasping attitude and its derivatives like hatred and so forth—dissolve into the indestructible drop. Then, during the third repetition, the imprints left by the defilements which are the obstructions to omniscience should be visualized in the form of many frightening insects. (It is funny, I find caterpillars very frightening!) You can visualize frightening insects coming from all directions and dissolving into the indestructible drop at your heart, and imagine that they sort of consume your precious body and mind. People generally find a scorpion very frightening; some even do not mention its name, just calling it "the negativities"![34] If such a visualization is done, it actually harms the self-cherishing attitude, because it brings about the experience of a threat to the sense of permanence and independence normally associated with our feeling of "I".

Having taken all the sufferings and defilements and so forth upon yourself, next develop the practice of compassion by giving. Give all the best qualities within yourself—your virtues, wealth, body and everything. They should be given to the other sentient beings without any sense of miserliness.

The practice of taking all types of sufferings can be extended by taking the obstructions to omniscience from the bodhisattvas at the high levels. Actually there is nothing you can take from those just on the point of actualizing enlightenment—but you can give your virtues so that they can increase the power of the antidotes for extinguishing the obstructions to omniscience. In the same way, you cannot take anything negative from your guru or from the Buddha, but there is something you can give. You cannot think that the guru and the buddhas are lacking happiness and that you can share your happiness, but rather, you can imagine your virtues in the form of offerings and then make these offerings to them.

96. THOUGH THE WORLD AND THE BEINGS THEREIN ARE FULL OF THE FRUITS OF EVIL, AND UNDESIRED SUFFERINGS SHOWER UPON ME LIKE RAIN,
INSPIRE ME TO SEE THEM AS MEANS TO EXHAUST THE RESULTS OF NEGATIVE KARMA, AND TO TAKE THESE MISERABLE CONDITIONS AS A PATH.

From here on, the text explains the practice of thought transformation. Most of the seven points of the seven-point thought transformation are included here. At this degenerated time, when we encounter adverse circumstances, we should be able to bring these factors into the context of the practice of bodhicitta. You should not let yourself fall under the influence of these circumstances, but rather should be determined that under any circumstances you will practice bodhicitta, whether you are sick or healthy. In both this lifetime and the future you must have the determination to carry on with the practice of bodhicitta. So, when you enjoy happiness you should dedicate it for the happiness of all the sentient beings.

97. IN SHORT, NO MATTER WHAT APPEARANCES
    MAY ARISE, BE THEY GOOD OR BAD,
    INSPIRE ME TO TAKE THEM INTO A PATH EN-
    HANCING THE TWO BODHICITTAS
    THROUGH THE PRACTICE OF THE FIVE
    FORCES—THE ESSENCE OF THE ENTIRE
    DHARMA—
    AND THUS ENJOY ONLY A MIND OF HAPPINESS.

This passage explains how to undertake a lifetime's practice on a daily basis. It explains what are called the five forces:

1) The force of intention. This is the intention to engage in an activity. When you wake up in the morning, you must develop the intention: Throughout this day I shall engage in the proper practice of bodhicitta, especially training in the attitude of exchanging myself for others. This is the preparation.

2) The force of familiarity. As explained before, the power of the virtuous qualities of the mind depends on familiarity with them. Just visualizing and meditating once will not help much. So, when you meet suffering sentient beings you should recall this practice. Actually, all circumstances should remind one of the practice of bodhicitta; that is what is meant by the force of familiarity. This is very important for all practices.

3) The force of meritorious deeds. This refers to engaging

in meritorious deeds in order to increase the practice of bod-hicitta.

4) The force of rejection, which is refraining from ill deeds.

5) The force of aspiration. When you go to bed you should dedicate all the merits, especially from the practice of bod-hicitta, for the welfare of all sentient beings.

Trying to integrate these forces each day is how you should go about doing your practice. Such a yogin's state of mind would not be disturbed by any external circumstances, whether they be favorable or adverse.

98. INSPIRE ME TO IMMEDIATELY CONJOIN WHAT-
    EVER I MEET TO MEDITATION
    BY THE SKILLFUL MEANS OF HAVING THE
    FOUR APPLICATIONS,
    AND TO MAKE THIS OPPORTUNE REBIRTH
    WORTHWHILE
    BY PRACTICING THE ADVICE AND COMMIT-
    MENTS OF MIND TRAINING.

This passage talks of employing four actions. These are:

1) accumulating merits; 2) purifying negative actions; 3) offering tormas to the harmful spirits; and 4) entrusting the dharma protectors with activities. Here one is requesting the harmful spirits to inflict more harms upon oneself, because if they do, it affects one's self-cherishing attitude—normally we would ask them not to disturb us. Here it also mentions requesting activities of the dharmapalas in order to have a very successful practice of thought transformation. The text then goes on to explain the eighteen commitments of thought trans-formation and the precepts of thought transformation practice.

Eight Verses on Thought Transformation
I shall now read and explain briefly one of the most impor-tant texts on thought transformation, *Lojong Tsigyema* (Eight Verses on Thought Transformation). It was composed by Geshe Langri Tangba, who was a very unusual bodhisattva. I myself

read it daily and received the transmission of the commentary from Kyabje Trijang Rinpoche.

(i) With a determination to accomplish
the highest welfare for all sentient beings,
Who surpass even a wish-granting jewel,
I will learn to hold them supremely dear.

One is requesting: May I be able to view them as a precious jewel because they are the object on whose account I can achieve omniscience; so, may I be able to hold them dear.

(ii) Whenever I associate with others, I will learn
to think of myself as the lowest among all,
And respectfully hold others as being supreme,
From the depth of my heart.

"Respectfully hold others as being supreme" means not regarding them as some object of pity that you look down on, but rather taking them as higher objects. Take, for example, insects: They are inferior to ourselves because they do not know the proper things to adopt and discard—whereas we do know because we see the destructive nature of the defilements. Such is the case, but we can look at the facts from another viewpoint as well. Although we are aware of the destructive nature of the defilements, we nevertheless let ourselves be under their influence, and in that sense we are inferior to insects.

(iii) In all actions, I will learn to search into my own mind,
And as soon as an afflictive emotion arises,
Endangering myself and others,
I will firmly face and avert it.

When one is engaged in a practice of this kind, the only thing which causes obstacles is the defilements within one's own mental continuum; on the other hand, spirits and so forth do not cause any obstacles. So, you should not have an attitude of idleness and passivity towards the inner enemy; but rather, you should be alert and forthcoming, countering the defilements immediately.

(iv) I will cherish beings of bad nature,

And those oppressed by strong negativities and sufferings,
As if I had found a precious treasure
Very difficult to find.

These lines emphasize the transformation of those thoughts focused on sentient beings who have very strong negativities; generally speaking, it is more difficult to have compassion towards persons afflicted by sufferings and so forth, when they have a very bad nature and personality. Actually, such people should be regarded as the most supreme objects of one's compassion. Your attitude, when you encounter such persons, should be as though you had found a treasure.

(v) When others, out of jealousy, treat me badly
With abuse, slander and so on,
I will learn to take all loss
And offer the victory to them.

Generally speaking, if others have done you wrong without any justification, it is—in worldly terms—lawful to retaliate; but the practitioner of thought transformation techniques should always give the victory to others.

(vi) When one whom I have benefited with great hope
Unreasonably hurts me very badly,
I will learn to view that person
As an excellent spiritual guide.

Then, regarding sentient beings for whom you have done a lot, normally you expect them to repay your kindness and thus you place hope in them. But instead, you should think: If such a person harms me instead of repaying my kindness, may I not retaliate against him, but rather reflect upon his kindness and be able to see him as a special guide.

(vii)In short, I will learn to offer to everyone without exception
All help and happiness directly and indirectly,
And secretly take upon myself
All the harms and suffering of my mothers.

It says, "In short, may I be able to offer all the good qualities that I have to all the sentient beings,"—this is the practice of giving—and, "May I be able secretly to take all their harms and sufferings of this and future lifetimes." This refers to the process of inhalation and exhalation.

Up to here, the verses have dealt with the practice of the conventional bodhicitta. The techniques for cultivating the conventional bodhicitta should not be influenced by attitudes such as: If I undertake the practice of giving and taking I will have better health, and so forth, which would indicate the influence of worldly considerations. You should not have the attitude: If I do such a practice people will respect me and regard me as a good practitioner. In short, your practice of these techniques should not be influenced by any worldly motives.

(viii)I will learn to keep all these practices
    Undefiled by the stains of the eight worldly conceptions,
    And, by understanding all phenomena to be like illusions,
    I will be released from the bondage of attachment.

These lines speak about the practice of ultimate bodhicitta. When we talk of the antidotes to the eight worldly attitudes, there are many levels. The actual antidote for overcoming the influence of such worldly attitudes is to understand the non-inherent nature of phenomena. All phenomena are not inherently existent—they are like illusions. Although they appear as truly existent they have no reality. "Having understood their relative nature, may I be freed from the binding knot of the self-grasping attitude."

You should read *Lojong Tsigyema* every day to enhance your practice of the bodhisattva ideal.

99. SO THAT I MAY RESCUE ALL BEINGS FROM THE VAST OCEAN OF BECOMING, INSPIRE ME TO MASTER TRUE BODHICITTA, THROUGH LOVE, COMPASSION AND THE SUPERIOR INTENTION CONJOINED WITH THE TECHNIQUE OF MOUNTING TAKING AND GIVING UPON THE BREATH.

Having done the visualization of the lojong practice, you should visualize the nectars descending and so forth.

100. INSPIRE ME TO EAGERLY STRIVE IN THE
     PRACTICE
     OF THE THREE MORALITIES OF THE MA-
     HAYANA,
     AND TO BIND MY MINDSTREAM WITH PURE
     BODHISATTVA VOWS,
     THE SINGLE PATH JOURNEYED BY VICTORI-
     OUS ONES OF THE THREE TIMES.

This verse deals with the bodhisattva vows. I think that at this point one can take bodhisattva vows on the basis of this manual, because the preliminaries such as refuge, confession, and so on, have been completed. Taking the vows can now be done by meditating on the verse "Sangye Choetsogma":

> I go for refuge to Buddha, dharma and the supreme com-
> munity
> until my achievement of complete enlightenment;
> Through the merits of giving and so forth that I have ac-
> quired,
> May I achieve buddhahood to help sentient beings,

or, the verse from the *Bodhisattvacharyavatara*:

> Just as the previous sugatas generated the precious bod-
> hicitta
> And practiced in accordance with its precepts,
> So shall I, in order to benefit all beings,
> Develop that precious mind and follow its precepts.

If you wish to cultivate the aspirational aspect of the bodhicitta you should do it at this point.

The next stanzas explain the six perfections. The four ripening factors are included within the six perfections. Here a review is made of the six perfections.

101. INSPIRE ME TO TRANSFORM MY BODY,
     WEALTH AND VIRTUES OF THE THREE
     TIMES
     INTO THE OBJECTS DESIRED BY EACH SEN-
     TIENT BEING;
     AND THROUGH THE ADVICE OF ENHANCING
     DETACHED GIVING,
     COMPLETE   THE   PERFECTION   OF
     GENEROSITY.

This first of these verses talks of the practice of generosity.
The possessions that you can afford to part with should be
given away with generosity, but the most important thing is
to increase and develop the attitude of generosity.

102. INSPIRE ME TO COMPLETE THE PERFECTION
     OF MORAL CONDUCT
     BY WORKING FOR SENTIENT BEINGS, AC-
     CUMULATING VIRTUOUS QUALITIES,
     AND NOT TRANSGRESSING THE BOUNDS OF
     THE PRATIMOKSHA,
     BODHICITTA OR TANTRIC VOWS, EVEN AT THE
     COST OF MY LIFE.

This passage speaks of the practice of the three types of morality; of restraint, of gathering virtues, and of working for the
welfare of others.

103. SHOULD ALL THE NINE TYPES OF BEINGS OF
     THE THREE REALMS
     BECOME ANGRY AT ME, ABUSE, UPBRAID,
     THREATEN, OR EVEN KILL ME,
     INSPIRE ME TO COMPLETE THE PERFECTION
     OF PATIENCE
     AND, UNDISTURBED, WORK FOR THEIR BEN-
     EFIT IN RESPONSE TO THEIR HARM.

The practice of patience: "Even if all the sentient beings arise as my enemy and take my life, may I be able to restrain myself from retaliating and losing my patience." The verse also explains the other types of patience such as those developed by voluntarily accepting suffering and through conviction in the dharma.

104. EVEN IF I MUST REMAIN IN THE FIRES OF AVICI
FOR AN OCEAN OF EONS FOR THE SAKE OF EACH SENTIENT BEING,
INSPIRE ME TO COMPLETE THE PERFECTION OF JOYOUS EFFORT,
AND THROUGH COMPASSION TO STRIVE FOR SUPREME ENLIGHTENMENT.

This speaks of the practice of joyous effort: "Through the force of compassion may I never lose the courage to work for the attainment of supreme enlightenment for the benefit of others."

105. BY AVOIDING THE FAULTS OF DULLNESS, AGITATION, AND DISTRACTION,
WITH ONE-POINTED CONCENTRATION SET ON
THE MODE OF EXISTENCE OF ALL PHENOMENA—VOIDNESS OF TRUE EXISTENCE—
INSPIRE ME TO COMPLETE THE PERFECTION OF CONCENTRATION.

This passage explains the practice of meditative stabilization: "May I be able to overcome mental sinking and mental excitement, which are the internal obstacles to concentration." Here the object taken for meditative stabilization is emptiness; an analytic process having been applied, absorptive meditation is undertaken. This is what is meant by searching for the absorptive meditation through the analytic process.

106. THROUGH THE WISDOM DISCRIMINATING
SUCHNESS
CONJOINED WITH THE INDUCED TRANQUIL-
ITY AND GREAT BLISS,
INSPIRE ME TO COMPLETE THE PERFECTION
OF WISDOM
THROUGH THE SPACE-LIKE YOGA ABSORBED
ON THE ULTIMATE TRUTH.

Here the perfection of wisdom is explained. The wisdom dis-
tinguishing the nature of phenomena—when assisted by the
factors of mental and physical pliancy arising after a realization of emptiness—could then engage in the yoga of space-
like meditative equipoise.

107. INSPIRE ME TO PERFECT THE ILLUSION-LIKE
CONCENTRATION
BY REALIZING HOW ALL OUTER AND INNER
PHENOMENA
LACK TRUE EXISTENCE YET STILL APPEAR
LIKE ILLUSIONS, DREAMS, OR THE MOON'S
IMAGE IN A STILL LAKE.

Regarding one's practice in the period subsequent to the attainment of equipoise, the verse says that although all
phenomena, both external and internal, lack inherent existence,
they still appear; they are just like reflections. Although they
do appear to be objectively existent, there is no such existence.
Their existence is only on the nominal level. So, you should
have the conviction: Although at this stage things do appear
to me as inherently existent, since I have had the experience
of their emptiness during meditative equipoise, I know they
are all like illusions. This explains the illusion-like meditation
of the post-meditational period.

108. SAMSARA AND NIRVANA HAVE NOT AN ATOM
OF TRUE EXISTENCE,

WHILE DEPENDENT ARISING BY CAUSE AND
EFFECT IS NON-DECEPTIVE;
INSPIRE ME TO REALIZE THE IMPORT OF
NAGARJUNA'S THOUGHT:
THAT THESE TWO ARE NOT CONTRADICTORY,
BUT COMPLEMENTARY.

These lines explain the seeing of emptiness in terms of dependent arising, and dependent arising in terms of emptiness; it is through the reasoning of dependent arising that one establishes emptiness. Because it is not independent, emptiness itself is also not inherently existent. The text explains that conventional reality, appearance, and the final mode of existence, emptiness, are complementary to each other. So, when you develop ascertainment of the infallibility of the law of interdependence, you will know that things are dependent upon other factors and they lack an independent nature. Therefore, you will be able to perceive that the appearance and the actual status are not contradictory, but rather, are complementary.

IV. THE STAGES OF THE TANTRIC PATH

109. THEN, THROUGH THE KINDNESS OF MY
      HELMSMAN, VAJRADHARA,
      INSPIRE ME TO CROSS THE LABYRINTH
      OCEAN OF TANTRA
      BY HOLDING MY VOWS AND PLEDGES, THE
      ROOT OF SIDDHIS,
      DEARER THAN MY LIFE.

This passage explains the practice of tantra: "Having taken the initiation, may I be able to observe the vows and commitments taken at that time."

110. INSPIRE ME TO CLEANSE ALL STAINS OF AT-
      TACHMENT TO ORDINARY APPEARANCE

> THROUGH THE FIRST STAGE YOGA OF TRANS-
> FORMING BIRTH, DEATH AND BARDO
> INTO THE THREE CONQUERORS' BODIES,
> AND TO SEE WHATEVER APPEARS AS THE
> DEITY.

This verse deals with the practice of the generation stage. The object of abandonment of the generation stage is the ordinary conception and appearance. There are two positions: One holds that according to tantra these two, ordinary conception and appearance, are actually the two obstructions; the other asserts that ordinary appearance and ordinary conception are the object of abandonment in the context of tantra on the generation stage. At least during the meditation session you should prevent yourself from falling under the influence of ordinary appearance and conception. Realization of the generation stage matures the practitioner for the practice of the completion stage.

111. SETTING YOUR FEET, O PROTECTOR, IN THE
>   EIGHT PETALS OF MY HEART
> WITHIN THE CENTRAL CHANNEL, INSPIRE
>   ME TO ACTUALIZE
> THE PATH UNITING CLEAR LIGHT AND ILLU-
>   SORY BODY
> IN THIS VERY LIFETIME.

To explain this in the context of Guhyasamaja, through the "subtle yoga of analysis" and the "gross yoga of single mindfulness" one can experience the isolated body and the isolated speech, which lead on to the isolated mind. On the stage of isolated mind, having received the inspiration of the Lama Lozang Thubwang Dorje Chang, the guru remains in the indestructible drop at the heart channel-wheel of yourself as the guru-deity.

The practice of completion stage, if you are undertaking it in particular, should be done at this point.

It is said that all virtuous practices are done on the basis of guru yoga. If you are undertaking your practice within such a framework, you should recite *Lama Choepa* at the beginning of the day, but the merit field should not be dissolved. You should do your other daily practices and other activities during the day, and when you go to bed you can dissolve the merit field and conclude *Lama Choepa*. As the guru dissolves into you, imagine that your body, speech and mind are blessed by the guru; being so greatly fortunate, you should enter into the clear light of sleep. When you arise in the morning, imagine arising from this clear light.

So, you can leave it either at this point or at a later stage (before verse 115). Leaving *Lama Choepa* at this point is at least honest, because you are saying to the merit field, "I have done some virtuous things and also I have done some non-virtuous things," and so you are making an honest declaration. There is actually such a tradition, which I think is very good. You can leave it at this point; I leave it here myself and do all my daily practices, sadhanas and so on in between. The whole purpose of practicing sadhanas is to achieve enlightenment in this lifetime. It is better to do the practices which follow later in this text, such as phowa (the transference of consciousness) and so forth, which are the practices of last resort, at the end of the day when you are going to bed. Prior to that you will have done all the other techniques such as sadhanas and so forth, which means that you have done your best.

112. SHOULD I NOT HAVE COMPLETED THE
POINTS OF THE PATH AT THE TIME OF
DEATH,
INSPIRE ME THAT I MAY REACH A PURE LAND
BY EITHER
THE INSTRUCTIONS ON APPLYING THE FIVE
FORCES, OR BY
THE FORCEFUL MEANS TO ENLIGHTENMENT,
THE GURU'S TRANSFERENCE.

The practice of phowa, the transference of consciousness, is

172 The Union of Bliss and Emptiness

mentioned here, as are the five forces, explained earlier. Here their meanings are specific to the time of death.

1) The force of intention: at the point of death to have the intention not to separate from bodhicitta.

2) The force of familiarity: to acquaint oneself with the stages of the dissolution related to the experience of death. Then, because of your training, when you actually experience them you will be able to recognize them without any obstructions. This has to be done through constant familiarization.

3) The force of the virtuous seed: giving up all one's material possessions by making offerings to the higher objects. At the time of death you should not have any attachment focused upon your relatives, possessions and so forth. This is very important; you have to be very clear about it. The more you actually dispense with possessions, the better you will feel.

4) The force of the antidote: the practices of self-initiation and other forms of purification.

5) The force of aspiration: that either at the time of death or after death during the intermediate state, one should make the aspirational prayer: May I never be separate from the bodhicitta even at the point of death, during my intermediate state, and so on.

If you are specializing in the practice of transference of consciousness, you can transform Lama Lozang Thubwang Dorje Chang into Amitabha, or you can focus your attention on the Amitabha in the merit field and invite him to your crown. Visualize your central channel, broader towards the tip and narrower at the lower end. The indestructible drop should be visualized in the form of white syllable A, and at the upper end of the channel you should visualize Amitabha, facing the same way as yourself. Visualize also the central channel of the deity, the lower end of which joins the upper end of your own central channel. Focusing upon the seed syllable at your heart, cultivate the desire to spring it upwards and shoot it into the heart of Amitabha at your crown. When you are training in the transference of consciousness, you have to draw the indestructible seed down again. You will reach a stage in this process

where you feel some kind of itching sensation at your crown—
that is the sign that you are actually trained. But at the time
of death you will not draw back the seed syllable, but rather
keep on shooting it up. All these visualizations are found in
commentaries on the transference of consciousness.

You should have a very good acquaintance with the dissolution process as explained in the Guhyasamaja tantra—the dissolution of the twenty-five gross phenomena and so forth. If
you experience death with a virtuous state of mind, such as
with the understanding of emptiness, strong faith in the guru,
and so forth, even though you might have indulged in negative actions during your life, the force of that temporary cir-
cumstance will have a great effect in determining your rebirth.

113. IN SHORT, O PROTECTOR, INSPIRE ME
    THAT I MAY BE CARED FOR BY YOU INSEPARA-
      BLY IN ALL MY FUTURE LIVES,
    AND BECOME THE CHIEF OF YOUR DISCIPLES,
    HOLDING EVERY SECRET OF YOUR BODY,
    SPEECH AND MIND.

114. O PROTECTOR, PLEASE GRANT ME THE GOOD
      FORTUNE TO BE
    THE VERY FOREMOST OF YOUR RETINUE
      WHEREVER YOU MANIFEST BUDDHAHOOD,
    AND THAT ALL MY TEMPORAL AND ULTI-
      MATE WISHES AND NEEDS
    BE EFFORTLESSLY AND SPONTANEOUSLY
    FULFILLED.

If you are practicing lamrim specifically, at this point you
should insert the request prayer.

7 Dissolving the Merit Field

Now for the dissolution of the merit field at the conclusion of the practice. Visualize that the lineage gurus dissolve into the root guru, the lineage gurus of the vast and profound practices into Maitreya and Manjushri, and those of the experiential lineage into Vajradhara, so that finally there are five gurus. Maitreya dissolves into the right arm of Lama Lozang Thubwang Dorje Chang, Manjushri into the left, Vajradhara into the crown, the root guru into the heart. The merit field dissolves from above and below into Lama Lozang Thubwang Dorje Chang who descends to your crown. Then visualize nectars descending, and make requests to him. It is very good to meditate on lamrim with that visualization.

115. HAVING BEEN THUS ENTREATED, PRAY
    GRANT THIS REQUEST, O SUPREME GURUS,
    SO THAT YOU MIGHT BLESS ME, HAPPILY
    ALIGHT ON THE CROWN OF MY HEAD
    AND ONCE AGAIN SET YOUR RADIANT FEET
    FIRMLY
    AT THE COROLLA OF MY HEART LOTUS.

Again make fervent prayers from the depth of your heart. Just as found in the lineage guru prayer of mahamudra practice:

> This body of mine and your body, O Father,
> This speech of mine and your speech, O Father,
> This mind of mine and your mind, O Father—
> Through your inspiring strength transform my three doors
> to become inseparable from yours.

Make fervent and strong prayers to the guru to be inseparable from you; the guru consents to your request and dissolves into you. Think that he will remain at your heart until your achievement of full enlightenment, blessing your heart. In some writings it has been explained that one should visualize the heart in the form of an eight-petalled lotus. You can visualize the guru entering into the lotus and the lotus closing its petals, and yourself becoming inseparable from the guru. As found in the commentaries on Yamantaka, it is also good to seal the lotus by what are known as the six seals.[35]

8 Dedication

116. I DEDICATE THE MERIT THUS GATHERED
     TOWARDS THE REALIZATION OF AIMS AND
     DEEDS
     OF BUDDHAS AND THEIR CHILDREN OF
     THREE TIMES,
     AND TO THE UPHOLDING OF THE DOCTRINE
     OF SCRIPTURE AND INSIGHT.

117. MAY I IN ALL LIVES, THROUGH THE FORCE OF
     THIS MERIT,
     NEVER SEPARATE FROM THE FOUR WHEELS
     OF THE GREAT VEHICLE
     AND ACCOMPLISH ALL THE STAGES OF THE
     PATH,
     RENUNCIATION, BODHICITTA, PERFECT VIEW
     AND THE TWO STAGES.

That is how you should undertake your daily practice over the
days, months, and years. It is good if you can actually gain
some realizations within this lifetime. Even if you cannot, this
practice will leave a very strong imprint within your mental
continuum.

Notes

1. The seven features of the deity and his consort facing each other are: 2) complete enjoyment; 2) union; 3) great bliss; 4) non-inherent existence; 5) great compassion; 6) uninterrupted continuity; and 7) non-cessation.

2. Panchen Lozang Choekyi Gyaltsen (1570-1662) was the first Panchen Lama and was a very influential figure in the Gelug tradition. His greatest impact was on the practical aspect of the doctrine, and the many texts that he left as his legacy still stand out for their clarity and comprehensiveness. He also served as the main tutor of H. H. the Fifth Dalai Lama.

3. When the practitioner has withdrawn all the gross levels of winds into the central channel and has thus ceased the conceptions they propel, he or she assumes a very subtle body having specific characteristics. Such a body is called illusory body (*gyu lu*) and also the enjoyment body of the path. It is the factor that purifies the intermediate state (*bardo*).

4. Clear light is the subtlest level of mind, which becomes manifest only when all the gross minds have ceased their active functions. This state is experienced by ordinary beings naturally at the time of death, but can also be intentionally induced through meditative techniques. The reference here is to the latter.

5. Truth body (*dharmakaya*), enjoyment body (*sambhogakaya*) and emanation body (*nirmanakaya*).

6. The twenty-five gross phenomena are: five aggregates, four elements, six sense faculties, five sense objects within one's continuum, and five basic wisdoms.

7. This refers to a process of gradual generation into a deity by the practitioner.

8. Isolations of body, speech and mind. Aided by the perception of every appearance as a mere sport or play of the "inseparable bliss and emptiness" in the completion stage, the practitioner mentally isolates his body, speech and mind from the tendencies of ordinariness.

9. The four complete purities are the features that distinguish the tantric path from that of the sutra. They are: complete purities of 1) environment; 2) body; 3) resource; and 4) deeds. For an explanation, see *Tantra in Tibet*, by H.H. Dalai Lama, Tsong-ka-pa and Jeffrey Hopkins, Snow Lion Publications, 1987.

10. Generation stage (*kerim*) and completion stage (*zogrim*).

11. See p. 66.

12. The seven features of the Vairochana posture are the positions of the following parts of the body, as discussed in the commentary: 1) legs; 2) hands; 3) shoulders; 4) spine; 5) head; 6) lips and teeth; and 7) tongue.

13. The term *mahayanist* has two different connotations, one from a philosophical viewpoint and the other from a practical perspective. The general reference is the latter one, for it is on the basis of the mental faculties of practitioners that the distinction between the great and lesser vehicles is made.

14. Detailed discussion on these reasonings can be found in the buddhist logical texts such as *Pramana-samura* by Dignaga and *Pramanavartika* of Dharmakirti. The logical premise of such reasonings is that however weak one's initial understanding of impermanence and selflessness is, if pursued with the right meditative techniques, it will eventually lead to direct experience. Because such understanding is rooted in a valid support of the mind, unlike athletic prowess, once de-

veloped it has the potential to come about spontaneously.

15. See p. 165.

16. The four immeasurables are: immeasurable compassion, love, joy and equanimity.

17. The dissolution process of entirety is a meditation on dissolving one's body into emptiness, where one visualizes the entire body melting into light and then dissolving both from above and below into the indestructible drop at the heart. Eventually the subtle drop is also dissolved into emptiness.

18. Diamond sliver reasoning is a form of reasoning heavily employed by Nagarjuna and his followers to refute the inherent existence of phenomena. A standard syllogism of this type of argument would read: A flower is not inherently produced because it is not self-produced, nor produced from inherently existing others, nor from both, nor causelessly. For a detailed explanation, see *Meditation on Emptiness*, by Jeffrey Hopkins, Wisdom Publications, 1983, pp. 57, 131 and 639.

19. The tree of the merit field is composed of seven precious materials. The root is gold; trunk silver; branches lapis lazuli; leaves crystal; stems turquoise; flowers red pearl; and fruit diamonds. This description is according to Yongzin Yeshe Gyaltsen's *Lama Choepa* commentary.

20. See *Abhisamayalankara* by Maitreya, chapter one.

21. The four factors for ripening the mind of others are: giving material aid; using gentle speech; teaching specific practices; and setting a perfect example through one's own way of life.

22. The four types of *vajrasanas* are those of legs, channels, winds and drops.

23. A reality source (*dharmodhya* or *dharmadhatu*) is an upturned pyramid symbolizing emptiness; it is often seen under the feet of wrathful deities.

24. Kunrig is one of the principal deities of yoga tantra. He is normally white with one face and four arms. The practice of this deity is well known for its extensive and complex hand mudras and leg postures.

25. For an extensive discussion on this topic, see *Ab-*

hisamayalankara by Maitreya, chapter four, and its related commentaries.

26. See p. 132.

27. The ten qualifications of a mahayana teacher as outlined in Maitreya's *Mahayana-sutralankara* are: 1) ethical self control; 2) serenity, meditative stabilization; 3) mental peace, derived through wisdom; 4) more knowledge than the disciple; 5) enthusiasm in practice; 6) richness of scriptural learning; 7) realization or reality; 8) skill in the art of teaching; 9) loving concern for the disciples; and 10) no sense of discouragement while working for the disciples.

28. The two sets of ten principles as enumerated in *The Fifty Verses of Guru Devotion* are the ten outer and ten inner principles. The first ten are: skill in 1) the art and meditation of mandala; 2) meditative stabilizations; 3) hand mudras; 4) the art of sitting, such as *vajrasana*; 5) different leg postures; 6) recitations; 7) fire-burnt ritual; 8) offering rituals; 9) fierce activities; and 10) dissolution processes.

The ten inner principles are: skill in 1) the counteracting of hindrances through meditation on protection circles; 2) the preparation of mantra chakras; 3) the conferring of vase and secret initiations; 4) the conferring of wisdom awareness and word initiations; 5) the separation of foes from their protectors; 6) torma rituals; 7) various mantra repetitions; 8) fierce activities; 9) rites of consecration; and 10) rites of initiations.

29. The first lesson on elementary debate opens with a simple discussion on the divisions, classifications and definitions of colors.

30. The ten powers are: knowledge of 1) sources and nonsources; 2) actions and their fruitions; 3) the concentrations, meditative liberations, and so forth; 4) superior and non-superior faculties; 5) the varieties of inclinations; 6) the divisions of the eighteen constituents and so forth; 7) the paths leading to all forms of cyclic existence and solitary peace; 8) the remembrance of former states; 9) death, transmigration, and birth; and 10) contaminations and their extinction.

31. The practice of mixing is one of the main methods of

taking ordinary death, intermediate state and rebirth into the path as the truth body, enjoyment body and emanation body respectively. There are altogether nine rounds of mixing with three for each, during the waking state, dream state and the state of deep sleep. For a detailed explanation, see *Clear Light of Bliss* by Geshe Kelsang Gyatso, Wisdom Publicaitons, 1982, p. 100.

32. *Pramanavartika*, chapter two.

33. The ten non-virtuous actions are as follows: three actions of body—killing, stealing and sexual misconduct; four of speech—lying, divisive talk, harsh speech and senseless gossip; and three of mind—covetousness, harmful intent and perverted views. Restraining oneself from these actions constitute the ten positive or virtuous actions.

34. The Tibetan name for scorpion is *digpa ranyag*, the first word of which also means negativity.

Bibliography of Works Cited

Abhidharmakosha (Treasury of Knowledge) by Vasubhandu.

Abhisamayalankara (Ornament of Clear Realizations) by Maitreya.

Bhebum Ngonpo (Blue Scripture) by Potowa.

Bodhisattvacharyavatara (Guide to the Bodhisattva's Way of Life) by Shantideva, translated by Stephen Batchelor, Library of Tibetan Works and Archives, Dharamsala.

Chagchen Zindri (Notes on Mahamudra) by Keutsang Rinpoche. In volume II, Collected Works, Library of Tibetan Works and Archives, Dharamsala.

Chatu-Shataka Shastra (Four Hundred Verses on the Middle Way) by Aryadeva.

Chod Thardoe Depon (Chod, Helmsman of Those Seeking Liberation) by Panchen Lozang Choekyi Gyaltsen.

De Lam Martid (Practical Guide on the Stages of the Path) by Panchen Lozang Choekyi Gyaltsen.

Drange Namje Lekshe Nyingpo (The Discrimination of the Definitive and Interpretive Words of the Buddha) by Tsongkhapa. In Tsong Khapa's *Speech of Gold in the "Essence of True Eloquence"*, Robert A. F. Thurman, Princeton Library of Asian Translation, Princeton.

Geden Tenpa Gyepai Monlam (A Prayer for the Flourishing of Virtuous Doctrine) by Gungtang Tenpai Donme.

Guru Panchasika (The Fifty Verses of Guru Devotion) by Ashvagosha, Library of Tibetan Works and Archives, Dharamsala.

Jei Sangwai Namthar (The Secret Biography of Tsongkhapa) by Jamyang Choeje Tashi Paelden.

Jhangchub Lamrim Chenmo (Great Exposition of the Stages of the Path) by Tsongkhapa.

Jorchoe Kelsang Dringyen (Preparatory Practices: A Necklace for the Fortunate Ones) by Pabongka Dechen Nyingpo, Library of Tibetan Works and Archives, Dharamsala.

Kachem Lung Kurma (Throwing to the Winds the Legacy of Oral Instruction) by Geshe Tsultrim Nyima.

Lama Choepai Triyig Sangwai Ne Nampar Chewa Nyengyue Mengag Gyi Tezoe (A Commentary of Lama Choepa Revealing the Secret: The Treasury of Ear-Whispered Instructions) by Yongzin Yeshe Gyaltsen.

Lama Jangbod (Calling the Guru From Afar) by Pabongka.

Lamrim Nyamgurma (Songs of Spiritual Experience) by Tsongkhapa.

Lay Tsog (Ritual Manual) by Paelden Lhamoe.

Lojong Tsigyema (Eight Verses on Thought Transformation) by Geshe Langri Tangba. In *Kindness, Clarity and Insight*, the Fourteenth Dalai Lama, translated and edited by Jeffrey Hopkins, Snow Lion Publications, Ithaca.

Madhyamaka-mulakarika (Fundamental Treatise on the Middle Way) by Nagarjuna. In *Emptiness*, Frederick J. Streng, Abingdon Press, New York.

Madhyamakavatara (Guide to the Middle Way) by Chandrakirti.

Mahayana-sutralankara (Ornament of Mahayana Sutras) by Asanga and Maitreya.

Ngagrim Chenmo (Great Exposition on Tantra) by Tsongkhapa. Part I in *Tantra in Tibet*, Parts II and III in *Deity Yoga*, both by the Fourteenth Dalai Lama, Tsong-ka-pa and Jeffrey Hopkins, Snow Lion Publications, Ithaca.

Pancha-krama (Five Stages) by Nagarjuna.

Pindikrita Sadhana (Condensation of the Means of Accomplishment) by Nagarjuna.

Ratnavali (The Precious Garland) by Nagararjuna. In *The Buddhism of Tibet*, the Fourteenth Dalai Lama, translated and edited by Jeffrey Hopkins, Snow Lion Publications, Ithaca.

Thubten Jithor (Dusting the Buddha's Doctrine) by Khedup Rinpoche.

Thundrug Lamai Naljor (Six Session Guru Yoga) by Pabongka. In *The Kalachakra Tantra*, the Fourteenth Dalai Lama, translated by Jeffrey Hopkins, Wisdom Publications, London.

Tsashe Tikchen Rigpai Gyatso (An Elaborate Commentary on Madhayamaka-mulakarita: The Ocean of Reason) by Tsongkhapa. In *Ocean of Reason*, Jeffrey Hopkins, Library of Tibetan Works and Archives, Dharamsala.

Uma Chenmo (Great Exposition of the Middle Way) by Jamyang Shepa. In *Meditation on Emptiness*, Jeffrey Hopkins, Wisdom Publications, London.

Uma Gongpa Rabsel (Elucidation of the Intent: A Commentary on Madhyamakavatara), by Tsongkhapa.

Vajramala Tantra (Diamond Rosary Tantra).

Vinaya Sutra (Three Hundred Stanzas on Vinaya) by Sakyaprabha.

The majority of the above texts are not yet available in English. Those texts for which publication data are given are presented in translation in whole or in part in the indicated titles.

Index